Adventures in Fast Forward

Life, Love, and Work for the ADD Adult

Kathleen G. Nadeau, Ph.D.

Brunner/Mazel, *Publishers* • New York

This book is designed as a guide to understanding ADD: what it is, what it is not, and ways to accommodate it in various life settings. The information is meant to enhance the reader's coping skills and knowledge base; it is not meant to be used in place of a formal medical diagnosis or appropriate medical treatment.

Library of Congress Cataloging-in-Publication Data

Nadeau, Kathleen G.
    Adventures in fast forward: life, love, and work for the ADD adult / Kathleen G. Nadeau.
      p. cm.
    Includes bibliographical references and indexes.
    ISBN: 0-87630-800-0 (pbk.)
    1. Attention-deficit disorder in adults—Popular works.
  I. Title.
RC394.A85N33 1996   96-4027
616.85' 89—dc20   CIP

Published by
BRUNNER/MAZEL, INC.
19 Union Square West
New York, New York 10003

Manufactured in the United States of America

10 9 8 7 6 5 4 3 2 1

Contents

Foreword

Kathleen Nadeau has written an insightful and informative book for and about adults with Attention Deficit Disorder (ADD). Throughout the reader-friendly text, she addresses the various aspects of this "living disability" that contribute to shaping the lives of many individuals. Dr. Nadeau celebrates the assets that living with differences may endow and looks thoughtfully at ways to mitigate the difficulties to which adults with ADD are often vulnerable.

Adventures in Fast Forward was produced as a part of Dr. Nadeau's ongoing professional work in the field of ADD. For a number of years, she has studied the multidimensional features of this neurobiological disorder. As a part of her clinical practice, she has applied these findings to assist individuals with ADD in living more satisfying and productive lives. She is well-known for her contributions to the field as a lecturer and author of other materials on ADD. Consistent with her other print resources, in this text, Dr. Nadeau provides a concise overview of the current diagnostic criteria and assessment standards.

As a part of her perspective of ADD in adults, Dr. Nadeau is sensitive to the contributions of internal and external influences that interact with the genetic inheritance of individuals with ADD. Her text takes into account the impact of gender as well as the wide range of backgrounds, abilities, and personality types among the population of persons who have this disorder. While these issues complicate the conceptualization of ADD, Dr. Nadeau presents them for the reader in a clear and useful manner.

A significant percentage of the adult population experiences *life, love, and work* in *fast forward*. While experiencing difficulties related to their attentional "Achilles' heel," many of them live happy and successful lives. Dr. Nadeau describes these individuals as "actors" rather than "reactors" in life. Through her association with successful adults who are, or have become, "actors," Dr. Nadeau has observed shared characteristics among them that she calls their "success traits." These individuals have a strong desire for and commitment to achieving success. Through a self-determined process, they employ their personal strengths to live in a manner that enables them to use and enjoy their innate abilities. They are sensitive to their need for situations, jobs, and relationships that are a good fit for them. Many of the specific strategies of these "actors," described in the text, will be useful to readers in achieving their own goals.

In her chapter discussions of life, love, and work, Dr. Nadeau emphasizes the importance of recognizing and using existing assets and developing new skills in order to manage ADD symptoms. Her suggestions are offered in a manner that will motivate readers with ADD to inventory their situation. Some readers will try strategies for the first time, others will be remotivated to "try, try again."

In response to *Adventures in Fast Forward,* some adults with ADD may find themselves slowing down and reflecting on the nature of strategies that work for them, while others may consider ways in which they have achieved growth in the past. A number will think about the high cost of learning that has come through their difficult personal experiences or will note that living with ADD has taught them that managing symptoms is genuinely difficult and requires commitment and hard work. Some will recognize the strength they have gained by proactively taking responsibility for their actions and attitude, while still others will consider the role of good health care services and self-care in maintaining well-being. Finally, many will note the importance of working with others in a field or workplace that values one's style and perspective. These and others responses will aid in the implementation of Dr. Nadeau's suggestions and enable individuals to use them to build on previous useful learning.

Adventures in Fast Forward is a valuable resource for adults living with ADD or for the bookshelf of anyone interested in learning more about this disorder in the adult years. Topics addressed cover a comprehensive range of adult issues, from the college years to the senior years. For this reason, whether readers are members of "Generation X," the "Baby Boomers," or their parents, this text offers them pertinent information for their *life, love, and work.*

Mary McDonald Richard
Student Disability Services
University of Iowa

Acknowledgments

My thanks to the members of the Montgomery County CH.A.D.D. Adult ADD Support Group for their enthusiastic support of this project. Thanks also to the many adults with ADD with whom I have had the privilege to work over the past several years. I want to express special appreciation to the individuals who have allowed me to share their stories of triumph and failure in this book so that others may benefit from their experience.

I want to acknowledge Mitchell Berkowitz, Third Eye Photography, Bethesda, Maryland, for most of the photographs used throughout this book. The individuals who appear in these photographs are all members of the Montgomery County CH.A.D.D. Adult Support Group or are professionals who specialize in working with ADD adults.

Introduction

This book has been written to answer the questions that are asked most often by people who suspect they may have ADD, or who have been newly diagnosed with ADD, and to provide concrete, practical strategies to cope with dilemmas that arise because of ADD. The book's format emerged from my clinical practice and from the support group for adults with ADD that I organized several years ago. It is designed to be direct, brief, highly readable, and practical.

Since establishing a support group for adults, I have become very familiar with the range of questions asked by adults when they first learn about ADD. Some of those adults have not yet been diagnosed and want more information before they go through a more formal diagnostic process. Others are looking for basic information. What is it? Do I need to be tested? What kinds of medications are used in treating ADD in adults? How do I explain ADD to my spouse? To my friends and family? What's a good job for me if I have ADD? What are my rights at work? How do I learn to organize myself? Where can I find someone who can treat ADD in adults?

The book has been organized so that the reader can refer easily to a particular question for which he or she may be seeking an answer; the book's format also gives the reader easy access to information about a specific ADD concern that he or she can provide a spouse, physician, or employer.

EXPLAINING ADD: WHAT IS IT? HOW IS IT DIAGNOSED? HOW IS IT TREATED?

My intention in the first three chapters of this book is to provide the reader with brief, up-to-date, informative answers to these questions. The book begins with a chapter on the history of this recently recognized disorder, its definition, causes, and underlying neurobiology; the next chapter explores how adult ADD is diagnosed; treatment of ADD, including medication, education, psychotherapy, and coaching, is covered in the third chapter.

SOLUTIONS TO ADD: TOOLS, TIPS, AND STRATEGIES

The "solution" portion of this book is designed to address a wide range of life situations affected by ADD and to provide practical strategies and accommodations. These chapters deal with social skills, organizational skills, marriage, family, work, and school. There is also a special chapter on women's issues, addressing the struggles unique to women with ADD.

The final chapters emphasize self-advocacy, building community resources, and learning about assistive technologies that are helpful in managing ADD symptoms. The last chapter presents a series of success stories about adults with ADD ranging from their college through senior years. A Resource List at the end of the book includes information about books, newsletters, organizations, on-line services, and tapes and videos that deal with ADD.

Adventures in Fast Forward

Life, Love, and Work for the ADD Adult

1

Understanding Adult ADD

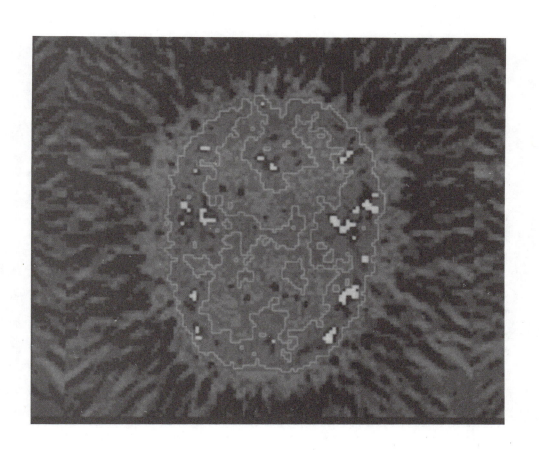

Understanding Adult ADD

What Is Adult ADD?

Our understanding of Attention Deficit Disorder keeps growing and changing. For years the disorder was known as "hyperactivity." The professional community thought that it was strictly a childhood disorder that was outgrown sometime during adolescence. By the late 1970s, researchers in the field became interested in other symptoms such as inattention and distractibility. Some children showed the symptoms of distractibility and inattention without being hyperactive. The focus then began to shift to an emphasis upon attentional problems. In 1980 the disorder was officially renamed Attention Deficit Disorder with two subtypes: ADD *with* and ADD *without* hyperactivity. Also in 1980, a new category, Attention Deficit Disorder–Residual Type, was added because some children continued to show attentional problems as they became adults. Despite this early recognition of "residual type" adult ADD in 1980, it was not until 1990 when Dr. Alan Zametkin published the first research article on adult ADD in a medical journal,* that a public awareness of ADD in adults really began to develop.

---

* All references to professional books and research articles are listed in the Reference Section at the end of the book. See the Resource List for books and information about ADD directed to individuals with ADD and to the general reader.

A photo of a PET (positron emission tomography) scan of an adult with ADD, similar to the one placed at the beginning of this chapter, was suddenly famous when it was featured in national news magazines. This PET scan demonstrated clearly for the first time that there were measurable differences in brain functioning in adults with ADD in comparison to non-ADD adults.

Throughout this book the term ADD is used to include all types of attention deficit disorders. The reader should note, however, that the "official" term used by the American Psychiatric Association is Attention Deficit/Hyperactivity Disorder (AD/HD). (Confusingly, even though the APA recognizes that some people with the disorder are not hyperactive, it continues to include the word hyperactivity even in the non-hyperactive subtype.) This chapter addresses only the official diagnostic criteria for AD/HD according to the American Psychiatric Association. Several adult ADD rating scales have been developed as well, including the "Utah Criteria" developed by Paul Wender's research group, and the Copeland Scale, developed by Edna Copeland, which address a broader range of symptoms than those listed by the American Psychiatric Association.

The official "definition" of Attention Deficit Disorder, along with the criteria for other disorders, is contained in the *Diagnostic and Statistical Manual of Mental Disorders* (DSM), published by the American Psychiatric Association. Periodically the DSM is revised, most recently in 1994. This latest version, the DSM-IV, presents us with changes in both the terminology and criteria for Attention Deficit Disorder. The DSM-IV refers to ADD as Attention Deficit/Hyperactivity Disorder, with three subtypes:

1. Predominantly *Hyperactive-Impulsive* Type

2. Predominantly *Inattentive* Type

3. *Combined* Type (meets criteria for both of the above)

The DSM-IV also allows the category *in partial remission* for adolescents and adults who no longer meet the full criteria for AD/HD of any subtype.

From the point of view of adults with ADD, the DSM-IV guidelines include two important changes in earlier definitions of ADD:

- There is clear recognition that Attention Deficit Disorder continues into adulthood.

- The *predominantly inattentive* subtype emphasizes more of the symptoms that are typically troubling for adults with ADD.

WHAT ARE THE SYMPTOMS OF ADD?

The following list of ADD symptoms follows the guidelines of the DSM-IV, but the wording has been adapted in some instances to be more descriptive of adults.

Inattention

- Distractibility
- Inattention to details (as in paperwork)
- Failure to complete tasks
- Poor planning ability
- Disorganization
- Resistance to tasks requiring an effort to concentrate
- Forgetfulness
- Tendency to lose or misplace personal items

Hyperactivity

- Feelings of restlessness
- Small-motor fidgeting—"nervous habits" such as toe tapping, drumming fingers
- Difficulty in quietly engaging in leisure activities
- Tendency to be talkative

Impulsivity

- Tendency to interrupt or intrude upon others
- Difficulty waiting one's turn in interactions with others

- Tendency to blurt out a response without waiting for the speaker to finish his or her question

The DSM-IV category *Combined Type* provides for categorization of individuals whose symptoms satisfy the criteria for both the inattentive and hyperactive-impulsive patterns.

AD/HD in Partial Remission

Six or more symptoms must be present for a diagnosis of ADD to be made; but if fewer symptoms are present, it is possible to make a diagnosis of AD/HD in *partial remission*. Many adults may tend to fall in the *partial remission* category.

In addition to the need for six symptoms, these are the other requirements for an AD/HD diagnosis:

- Symptoms are more frequent and severe than in others of similar age.
- Symptoms must have been present before age 7.
- Symptoms must be observed in more than one primary setting.
- Symptoms must interfere with academic, social, or occupational functioning.
- Symptoms are not the result of another disorder.

ARE THERE OTHER CHARACTERISTICS OF ADULT ADD?

The preceding section discussed only those symptoms included in the "official" symptom list of the DSM-IV. There are, however, many other problems and patterns seen in adults with ADD. Below is a brief list of some of these characteristics.

- Chronic forgetfulness
- Problems with time management
- Tendency to take on too many tasks at once

- General disorganization—late, rushed, unprepared
- Difficulty managing checkbook and finances
- Frequent moves and/or job changes
- Tendency to speak before considering consequences
- Difficulty controlling temper
- Difficulty managing paperwork
- Underachievement
- Tendency to seek "caretakers" to manage details of life
- Periodic depression (often begins in adolescence)
- Difficulty maintaining long-term relationships
- Tendency toward substance abuse
- Problems with decision making—either impulsive or obsessional
- Underactive, with a prior history of overactivity
- Low frustration tolerance
- Tendency to leave projects incomplete
- Pattern of short-lived interests
- Difficulty concentrating when reading
- Difficulty during intensive learning situations
- Thoughts tend to wander when listening to others
- Tendency to be a "night owl," with difficulty rising on time in the morning

Not all adults with ADD share all of these characteristics. The preceding list is not meant as a diagnostic tool, but rather is intended to briefly describe some of the cognitive, emotional, and behavioral patterns often seen in adults with ADD.

WHY WASN'T ADULT ADD RECOGNIZED EARLIER?

ADD is not a new disorder; it is a newly recognized disorder. The recent awareness of ADD in adults is the result of our increased understanding of ADD. The *Diag-*

nostic and Statistical Manual of Mental Disorders—Third Edition (DSM-III) recognized for the first time in 1980 that ADD, in some instances, continues into adulthood. The diagnostic category *Attention Deficit Disorder–Residual Type* (ADD-RT) was added to the DSM-III.

During the 1980s, Dr. Paul Wender and others at the University of Utah developed their own set of criteria for diagnosing adults with ADD and conducted a series of research projects. During this same period several longitudinal studies were undertaken, most notably by a group headed by Gabrielle Weiss and Lillian Hechtman, who described their work in the book *Hyperactive Children Grown Up*. Both groups, however, studied individuals whose characteristics conformed to the hyperactive subtype of ADD, ignoring perhaps the largest groups of adults with ADD, who fall into the predominantly inattentive category.

Despite this ongoing research, widespread awareness of ADD in adults did not exist. In the mid-1980s, active parents' groups began to form to advocate for the needs of children with ADD. At their meetings, many parents quickly realized that they shared many of the same characteristics seen in their ADD children. These adults began to refer to themselves as ADD adults. In this way, recognition of adult ADD, particularly including the nonhyperactive variant, piggybacked on the wave of concern for children with ADD.

In November 1990, an article was published in the *New England Journal of Medicine* that described a study of adults whose histories suggested AD/HD in childhood; it was conducted by Dr. Alan Zametkin of the National Institute of Mental Health. Zametkin's study suggested a physiological basis for AD/HD. Ironically, adults were studied not from a specific interest in adult issues, but because the low level of radiation emitted by the PET scans (positron emission tomography) used in the study was considered too risky for children. Adults eager for recognition of their disorder, and for help, embraced Zametkin's study, the first research that seemed to offer real "proof" of adult ADD. During that same month, at the national meeting of CH.A.D.D. (Children with Attention Deficit Disorder), a panel was organized to discuss ADD in adults.

In the few years since the first panel on adult issues was organized at a CH.A.D.D. annual meeting, the recognition of adult ADD has come a long way. CH.A.D.D., the largest national organization concerned with ADD, has officially changed its name to include "adults" in its title. ADDA, another large national group, focuses exclusively on the needs of ADD adults and their families. Support groups have sprung up all over the country, and several newsletters focusing on adult ADD have come into being. In the mid-1990s, adult ADD has received considerable media attention, greatly broadening the public's awareness. Through newspaper articles, magazine articles, and television features, many adults with ADD have learned of the disorder for the first time and have sought diagnosis and treatment.

WHAT IS THE MEDICAL EVIDENCE FOR ADD?

There is much that medical science does not yet understand about ADD. However, there is general agreement in the medical/neuroscience community that ADD is a neurochemical disorder.

As mentioned earlier, the first article describing medical evidence of a physiological basis for AD/HD was published by Dr. Alan Zametkin in 1990. Zametkin's research suggested that there was decreased glucose metabolism in areas of the brain that control attention and motor activity—the premotor cortex and superior prefrontal cortex. In other words, these areas of the brain did not receive enough fuel—glucose—and were therefore underfunctioning.

Subsequent research suggests that other areas of the brain are involved in AD/HD, including the corpus callosum, which connects the two hemispheres of the cortex, and the reticular activating system, which affects the brain's level of arousal, among other functions.

Since the early 1970s, many studies, both animal and human, have been conducted suggesting that impaired use of two neurotransmitters, dopamine (DA) and norepinephrine (NE), are involved in AD/HD. This faulty neurochemical system is believed to impair the functioning of the frontal lobes of the brain. Impaired ability of the brain to use DA and NE has been linked to impulsivity, hyperactivity, and some types of learning and memory impairments. The stimulant medications used to treat ADD increase the amounts of DA and NE available for use by the brain.

WHAT CAUSES ADD?

ADD tends to occur among close blood relatives, which has led to the common belief that there is probably a genetic basis for ADD. Dr. David Comings, a researcher in genetics, has studied ADD in relation to a number of other disorders including depression, alcoholism, and Tourette's Syndrome. Dr. Comings believes that there may be a genetic link among these disorders.

In a very small percentage of individuals, ADD symptoms may be due to a genetic thyroid disorder. Dr. Peter Hauser at the National Institute of Mental Health has conducted research linking ADD and hypothyroidism. The percentage of persons whose ADD is likely linked to thyroid malfunction is very small, however. Thyroid testing in relation to ADD should probably be undertaken only if there is a family history of thyroid problems.

A small but vocal minority of individuals believe that ADD is related to allergies. The majority of the scientific community does not support this position.

ADD is not a psychological reaction to poor parenting or lack of discipline. ADD symptoms are not the result of "laziness" or "lack of motivation," in the moralistic sense. It is true, however, that many individuals with ADD experience difficulties with motivation. Some scientists believe that there is a dysfunction in parts of the brain that control response–reward interactions so that individuals with ADD may be less responsive to both punishment and reward.

ADD-like symptoms may also result from prematurity, encephalitis, or exposure to toxins, such as lead, in early childhood. There is some evidence that ADD symptoms in a child may result from the mother's alcohol or drug abuse during pregnancy.

WHY WAS MY ADD NOT IDENTIFIED EARLIER?

There are a number of reasons that an individual can reach adulthood without receiving an ADD diagnosis. Unfortunately, some adults who are not diagnosed until adulthood face skepticism from employers, family members, and friends, who may suspect them of using the ADD diagnosis as a "medical excuse" for irresponsibility or disorganization. Here are the factors that may lead to delayed diagnosis.

Early Misunderstanding of Hyperactivity

Many adults who are now being diagnosed with ADD report vague memories of being "taken to a doctor" when they were in elementary school because they were "hyper." Knowledge of how to treat these children and how to help them in school was extremely limited; some children may have been placed briefly on Ritalin. However, our understanding of the disorder was minimal fifteen or twenty years ago. Even those children who were identified as being "hyper" weren't understood to have a lifelong disorder. Parents and pediatricians alike often assumed it was a minor, short-term behavior problem. Because hyperactivity is often reduced or "outgrown" during adolescence, few parents, teachers, or physicians realized that a whole host of symptoms continued into adulthood.

Inattentive ADD More Easily Overlooked

Most non-hyperactive children with ADD *(AD/HD, Predominantly Inattentive Type* according to the current nomenclature) were overlooked during their childhood because they did not present behavior problems at home or at school. Even those who were recognized as daydreamers were not viewed as having a neurobiological disorder. Children were simply admonished to "pay attention" and to "try harder."

Mild Symptoms

The squeaky wheel gets the oil. Children with more moderate symptoms were frequently overlooked. Boys who were only moderately hyperactive were likely to be viewed as simply "all boy." Likewise, children whose inattention was not extreme were not likely to be identified as being in need of help.

High Intelligence

Intelligence can have a profound effect upon how ADD symptoms are manifested. Many very bright adults report that in elementary school, even though they had much difficulty paying consistent attention to the teacher, it did not pose a problem. Schoolwork was not challenging for them, and they could count on the teacher to repeat important information many times. If they tuned out temporarily, they were likely to catch the information during a repetition.

Structured Home and School Environments

We are all aware now that structure is essential to good functioning for children with ADD. Some children with ADD had the good fortune to grow up in families that were highly structured and to attend schools that also provided a great deal of structure. Under such circumstances, children can much more easily compensate for ADD symptoms. One man recalled that his ADD wasn't clearly evident until his freshman year in college, when he suddenly was thrust into a completely unstructured environment. His ADD had been well managed—he grew up in a well-organized home and, for 12 years, attended a highly structured private school.

Misinterpretation of Symptoms

ADD symptoms can be very obvious, and yet go unrecognized because they are misinterpreted as "immaturity," "laziness," or "lack of motivation" by parents or teachers.

We know much more now about how ADD symptoms are seen in adults, and we are therefore more likely to make the diagnosis. But there is still need for improvement in the diagnosis of adults. Few professionals have received training in adult ADD issues, and few professionals routinely screen for ADD as part of an initial evaluation.

EXPLAINING ADD TO OTHERS

To People Who Think ADD Is "Just a Big Excuse!"

ADD is not an excuse; it's an explanation. ADD is a genuine neurobiological disorder that can cause a broad array of symptoms. As with people who have other types of disabilities, it is crucial that the adult with ADD not use his or her disability as a screen to hide behind. Having ADD means that you will be more challenged than others as you work to meet the demands of your life. This book is designed to help you meet that challenge.

People who wait to disclose their ADD until they are "in trouble" are very likely to be seen as using ADD as an excuse. Adults who "own" their ADD, who take charge of it and take responsibility for it, are much less likely to be viewed as using their ADD as an "excuse." The adult with ADD should work actively to develop coping strategies and to communicate those coping strategies to the people who are most affected by their ADD. Adults with ADD can convey a very responsible, positive approach by engaging in productive problem solving with the people in their lives who are affected by their ADD patterns.

Even when an adult with ADD takes a very proactive approach, he or she will probably encounter some detractors who don't "buy" the concept of Attention Deficit Disorder. If a detractor is a key player in the life of an adult with ADD, then attempts at education are in order. The adult with ADD may need to invite a boss or spouse to a consultation regarding the medical evidence for ADD as well as provide information on useful accommodations and coping strategies.

To People Who Say "Everyone Has Problems Like That!"

ADD is a disorder that can be difficult to accept and understand because many of the symptoms of ADD are common experiences for most of us. To some extent, almost everyone has acted impulsively, has been unable to concentrate, or has been messy and disorganized in some aspect of life. Because these are such "ordinary" problems, it is easy to confuse the occasional difficulties all of us have with the chronic and pervasive problems experienced by adults with ADD.

Those who believe that almost anyone could claim to have ADD need to understand that a diagnosis of Attention Deficit Disorder should never be made unless there is a cluster of symptoms that have been in evidence since early childhood and that significantly affect the individual's ability to function in some major life activity. ADD should never be casually tossed around as an "explanation" for mild absentmindedness or occasional disorganization.

ADD symptoms, just like the symptoms of many other disorders, exist along a continuum from mild to severe. Symptoms of anxiety and depression exist along a similar continuum. Because the public is more familiar with these disorders, it is perhaps easier to understand the differences between occasional mild anxiety and full blown panic attacks, or the difference between feeling blue and serious clinical depression. It may be helpful to use anxiety and depression as examples of well-recognized disorders that exist along a continuum. Just as a diagnosis of anxiety or depression is not made in response to occasional passing distress, a diagnosis of ADD is not made when someone experiences mild or transitory problems with distractibility or disorganization.

MYTHS ABOUT ADD

Unfortunately, many myths about ADD persist, based on misunderstandings about ADD or based on outdated notions about the disorder that have since been disproved. The adult ADD consumer needs to be aware, as he or she searches for a professional to treat ADD, that some misperceptions still exist in the professional community. Here are some of the more common misperceptions.

"If You Did Well in School, You Can't Have ADD."

This misunderstanding is based on the common stereotype that most people had of ADD until a few years ago—that of a hyperactive young boy who was disruptive in class, never did his homework, and presented behavioral problems at home, at school, and on the playground.

It is quite possible to do well in school despite ADD if you are non-hyperactive, have high intelligence, and have a reasonable degree of structured support at home and at school. ADD symptoms tend to appear at a time when the demands for performance from the environment exceed the individual's ability to function. For some people, this stage may not be reached until they are in the relatively unstructured but demanding academic environment of college or graduate school.

"If You Earned a Graduate Degree, You Can't Have ADD."

If you have been able to complete your education, you may run up against this stereotype when trying to obtain an evaluation and treatment for ADD. One man with a Ph.D. in a technical field reported that when he sought treatment for ADD symptoms, the psychiatrist he consulted told him point-blank, during their initial interview, that his Ph.D. was evidence that he did not have ADD! In fact, there are many very bright individuals with ADD or learning disabilities (LD), or both, who have successfully, through prolonged, painful effort, completed their graduate degree. Often these individuals find that they function far below their capacity in their chosen field of endeavor, and they struggle constantly against patterns of procrastination, distractibility, and disorganization.

An article in the Johns Hopkins Alumni Bulletin featured a brilliant paleobiologist who was diagnosed with ADD in his forties and who has had a very positive response to medication, including marked improvement in memory. It will take more articles such as this to begin to educate the professional community and the public about the very real plight of highly educated professionals who struggle with ADD.

"If You Respond Positively to Stimulant Medication, You Have ADD."

A positive response to stimulant medication does *not* mean that an individual has ADD. Ritalin and Dexedrine work much the way a cup of coffee does. Anyone who takes a stimulant will, to some extent, feel more focused and alert. Unfortunately, some less informed professionals continue to view a positive medication response as a "test" of ADD.

"All You Need to Treat ADD Is Medication."

Some individuals approach medication hoping for a magic bullet. Responses to medication are quite variable. Some people experience a dramatic difference, while others experience only modest improvement. There are those who experience a dramatic improvement temporarily but later report that long-term benefits of medication are greatly reduced.

Many factors are involved in consistent, successful functioning that cannot be provided by medication. Medication may create conditions under which more consistent, focused functioning is possible, but much habit building and learning needs to take place. For people who are not diagnosed until adulthood, much unlearning also needs to take place. A lifetime of ADD behavior often results in low self-esteem and a poor self-image, which need to be improved gradually and changed through psychotherapy.

"Stimulant Medications Are Dangerous."

All medications should be prescribed carefully, by a physician who is thoroughly informed about other health conditions and who is knowledgeable about ADD. But with this understood, just as for the treatment of any condition, the stimulant medications used to treat ADD are among the safest on the market. They are not new drugs. We have numerous longitudinal studies on the effects of stimulant medication. Much of the "bad press" received by Ritalin and Dexedrine has been generated by misinformed groups with rather extreme attitudes toward medication. For the vast majority of individuals, stimulants are safe, effective, and relatively free of side effects.

WHAT ADD IS *NOT:*

- An excuse

- Just a fad

- A myth

- Cured by "trying harder"

- Caused by poor parenting

- A politically correct term for "lazy" or "immature" behavior

WHAT ADD *IS:*

- A neurobiological condition

- Hereditary

- Often found in conjunction with other disorders, including depression, anxiety, and learning disabilities

- A condition that causes difficulties with impulse control, concentration, memory, organization planning, follow-through, and self-monitoring

- A condition that can vary widely in severity and symptoms

- Improved or worsened through stress level, lifestyle, and environment

- Best managed through a combination of medication, structured therapy, and by learning compensatory strategies and accommodations

Is There a Positive Side to ADD?

There are many positive aspects of ADD. Although the life challenges posed by ADD traits are very real and should not be denied, it is essential to celebrate your strengths and special gifts as well. A key to understanding and managing your ADD is to learn to celebrate the positive aspects of who you are, while being realistic about areas of difficulty.

Here is a list of positive ADD traits developed by members of an adult ADD support group. See if you can add more of your own!

Enthusiastic	Energetic
Good at finding novel solutions	Highly Verbal
Good in crisis situations	Spontaneous
Good at improvising	Creative
Can "think on their feet"	Fun to be around
Don't "stay mad" for long	Exciting

Recognizing and learning to emphasize the positive aspects of ADD is an essential part of reaching your potential as an adult with ADD. Learn what you're good at, recognize and appreciate your positive side, and look for people who can appreciate your positive side, too.

Try to arrange your life so that you are in a supportive environment, both in your personal life and at work. Think strategically, and work toward arranging an environment that allows you to use your best traits. People seek treatment for ADD in response to problems caused by ADD. An essential part of treatment for ADD, however, is to realize that ADD can be a plus in your life as well as a challenge. It is important that you choose to be around people, both in your personal life and in your work life, who appreciate those positive aspects and can support you in becoming your best self.

2

Diagnosing Adult ADD

Diagnosing Adult ADD

How Is ADD Diagnosed?

The starting point in any good diagnostic process for adult ADD should be a very thorough clinical interview that covers current problems as well as childhood, family, workplace, and educational issues. Some experts in the field of ADD believe that all that is needed for an adequate diagnosis is a clinical interview, while others believe that a thorough test battery is best. (These issues are discussed in greater detail later in this chapter.)

For a good diagnosis to be made with only a clinical interview, it is essential that the professional conducting the interview be thoroughly familiar with ADD, not only as it is manifested in childhood, but also in adulthood. It can be very difficult to find individuals with these qualifications.

It is also critical that the professional be thoroughly familiar with patterns found in nonhyperactive adults with ADD. The childhood history of such a person will be quite different from the history of someone who was hyperactive as a child. The clinician who is expecting a history of behavior problems and poor academic performance may entirely overlook the very subtle signs of predominantly inattentive ADD. These signs can be even more subtle if the individual in question has an above-average IQ.

Why Your Therapist Hasn't Diagnosed Your ADD

If you are currently in therapy, or have been in psychotherapy in the past, and have not been diagnosed with ADD, your experience is far from unique. But don't be too quick to judge your therapist! The recognition of adult ADD is so recent that very few therapists have received training to diagnose or treat this disorder. If your therapist is an adult therapist, chances are good that he or she has never received any training concerning ADD. Until recently, it was considered to be strictly a childhood disorder.

The first book for professionals exclusively focusing on the diagnosis and treatment of adults with ADD, *A Comprehensive Guide to Attention Deficit Disorder in Adults: Research, Diagnosis, and Treatment,* was not published until 1995.

If you are currently in therapy with someone who knows little about adult ADD, it may be useful to suggest some reading material to familiarize your therapist with adult ADD issues and treatment approaches. You may want to seek an adult ADD evaluation from someone who is more experienced with adult ADD and to ask this person to consult with your therapist regarding issues in adult ADD. It is also possible to work with a therapist, focused on adult ADD issues, on a short-term basis while continuing more extended therapy with your original therapist.

If you do elect to remain with a therapist who is not familiar with adult ADD issues, it is essential that your therapist become informed about adult ADD so that ADD traits and symptoms are not misinterpreted.

Why Shouldn't I Diagnose ADD Myself?

Many adults with ADD have "self-diagnosed" their ADD through reading articles and checklists. It is important to realize, however, that while your self-diagnosis may be completely accurate, it is never a good idea to rely solely on such a technique. This is because there is a long list of other disorders that share many symptoms with ADD. Only a highly trained clinician is qualified to make the sometimes subtle distinctions between ADD and these other disorders. Some of these disorders may coexist with ADD, while others may appear to be ADD but are something else entirely.

WHO IS QUALIFIED TO DIAGNOSE ADD?

There are a number of professionals in different fields who may be qualified to diagnose ADD. The most likely professionals to seek out are those who have worked in the field of ADD for many years treating children. In the past ten years or so, many of these people gradually have treated older children, as their patients grew up. Quite often, such professionals also began to work with the parents of children in their practice when those parents reported a history of ADD as a child or reported ongoing problems with ADD in adulthood.

Experienced professionals can be found in the fields of:

Pediatrics
Developmental Pediatrics
Clinical Psychology
Neuropsychology
Educational Psychology
Child Psychiatry
Adult Psychiatry
Neurology

FINDING A QUALIFIED PROFESSIONAL

Unfortunately, at this time there is no easy answer to this question. Very few professionals are experienced in treating ADD in adults, and most of those who have experience are clustered around universities or in metropolitan areas.

You may need to be prepared to travel some distance to receive diagnosis and treatment. If you live in a more remote area, you may need to travel for an initial evaluation, with periodic face-to-face meetings interspersed among telephone consultations.

There are different phases of diagnosis and treatment. You may need to travel long distances for an initial medication evaluation. Once you are following a satisfactory medication plan, a local physician may be willing to prescribe medication if you have periodic consultations with an ADD specialist.

You may need to see more than one professional during the course of your treatment for ADD. Your medication may be prescribed by a physician, while your psychotherapy, career counseling, or coaching might be provided by other professionals.

The best way to find out who knows about ADD in your neighborhood is by networking. Call a local elementary school to inquire about ADD organizations. Call ADDA (Attention Deficit Disorder Association) or CH.A.D.D. (Children and Adults with Attention Deficit Disorder) to inquire about the chapter nearest to you. There is also a growing network of adult ADD support groups. By attending any of these local meetings, you will have the opportunity to network with others to learn the names of respected ADD professionals in your community. There are also ADD bulletin boards on several on-line computer services. See the Resource List for phone numbers, addresses, and on-line bulletin board services.

Questions to Ask

- How long have you been treating adults with ADD?

- What proportion of patients that you treat are adults with ADD?

- Are you familiar with CH.A.D.D. and ADDA?

- Are you familiar with books on adult ADD published during the past several years? (See the Resource List and Reference Section for a list of books and articles on adult ADD.)

- Do you work with other professionals in the community who are experts in ADD?

- Have you given presentations on adult ADD in the community?

- Have you written any articles on adult ADD?

- Have you attended workshops or national conferences on adult ADD?

IS TESTING NECESSARY?

There is an important distinction between diagnosis and assessment of ADD in adults. A professional may be able to determine through a thorough interview that you show most of the symptoms of adult ADD. ADD rarely exists in a vacuum, however. There are a range of other important questions to answer, including coexisting psychological conditions such as anxiety and depression, as well as other cognitive and learning problems.

Testing can be very useful in an ADD evaluation for several reasons:

1. Test results can be helpful to confirm the presence of patterns reported by the individual in a clinical interview.

2. Testing can provide the examiner with an opportunity to observe a person under conditions that call for prolonged concentration and that require the person to use a variety of cognitive functions.

3. Testing can provide assessment of other psychological disorders likely to coexist with ADD.

4. Testing can offer an assessment of related cognitive problems including memory difficulties and learning disabilities.

5. Testing can establish a baseline measure of functioning to use for comparison in assessing ADD symptoms after treatment is underway.

6. Testing can assist in determining the proper medication or combination of medications that may be most effective.

7. Testing can help in the development of a treatment plan. Not all adults with ADD are identical in their symptom patterns and problem areas.

ASSESSMENT OF ADULT ADD

There is no *single* test for ADD. Beware of anyone who represents a particular test as the definitive measure of ADD! There are a number of computerized tests that have been designed to measure ADD traits (more about this later). Such tests are sometimes presented as an accurate measure of ADD. You, as the educated consumer, should know, however, that such tests should not be used alone to diagnose ADD but should only be used as part of a comprehensive evaluation.

Following is a thorough list of assessment procedures. First, you need to undergo a thorough screening interview, records review, and screening questionnaire focused on ADD. This should then be followed by a comprehensive test battery. You may not need all of the types of tests listed here—during the initial screening process, your examiner should decide on the most appropriate tests for you.

Interview

A thorough assessment for ADD should begin with a lengthy
includes questions about:

- Childhood history

- Medical history

- Educational history

- Employment history

- Family history

- Current functioning

Records Review

The examiner should review any records that are pertinent such as previous test
reports, report cards from childhood, or performance reviews from work. You
should bring any records that you may have at home. You will need to sign a
release form to allow the examiner to order records from physicians, therapists,
schools, employers, or any other source of information about your previous
functioning.

Screening Questionnaire

A number of questionnaires have been developed to evaluate adults for ADD.
Be sure—if you suspect that you have ADD *without* hyperactivity—that you are
not given a questionnaire that strongly emphasizes hyperactivity and impulsivity. Some early questionnaires strongly emphasize hyperactivity and under-
emphasize problems with attention and organization.

It can be very helpful to have a spouse, roommate, relative, or close friend
complete a questionnaire that describes you. Sometimes the people around you
have clearer perspectives than you do on your behavior.

Childhood ADD screening instruments can also be useful to fill out retro-
spectively. It can be helpful to ask one of your parents to complete a child ADD

questionnaire as they remember you during elementary school years. It may also be helpful for you to complete a child ADD questionnaire as you recall yourself during childhood.

Tests of Cognitive Functioning

Some cognitive tests that may be useful in measuring concentration, planning, organization, or memory include the following (only a sampling of the most commonly used tests of cognitive functioning):

> Wechsler Adult Intelligence Scale–Revised
> Wechsler Memory Scales–Revised
> Matching Familiar Figures–Adolescent/Adult Form
> Cancellation Task
> Wisconsin Card Sorting Test

Computerized Tests

Computerized tests have been developed to measure sustained attention and distractibility, such as the following:

> Test of Variables of Attention
> Gordon Diagnostic System
> Continuous Performance Test

As mentioned earlier, such tests should never be used as a "definitive" measure of ADD. It is quite possible to perform very well on these tests and yet have significant ADD symptoms in daily life. Unfortunately, some professionals operate under the misconception that these tests can "measure" ADD.

Tests for Learning Disabilities

Educational tests should be considered if learning disabilities are suspected. Many tests might be useful, depending on particular problem areas, difficulty with reading, writing, mathematics, verbal expression, verbal comprehension, and memory. One test that is very comprehensive and generally considered to be a standard part of an evaluation for learning disabilities is the:

>Woodcock-Johnson Psychoeducational Battery—Revised

Neurological Screening

Because symptoms of ADD may possibly be symptomatic of other neurological problems, a neurological screening questionnaire should be administered, or questions to screen for possible neurological concerns should be included in the initial interview. One such instrument, designed to screen for possible neurological problems, is the:

>Neurological Symptoms Questionnaire

Psychological Tests

Psychological problems such as anxiety and depression, as well as other conditions, commonly coexist with ADD in adults. A good test battery should include at least one general screening test such as the:

>Minnesota Multiphasic Personality Inventory–II
>Millon Clinical Multiaxial Inventory

If problems are suggested by test responses, then the examiner may want to administer a more complete psychological evaluation.

Another test that has proven quite useful as part of an assessment of Attention Deficit Disorder in adults is the:

>Myers-Briggs Type Inventory

The Myers-Briggs places an individual in one of 16 different personality types. Understanding your personality type, in combination with other factors, such as ADD, can be very helpful in formulating a treatment approach. It is important for both you and your evaluator not to become overfocused on the issue of ADD. Developing a good treatment approach depends on understanding many things about you in addition to answering a more specific question about whether or not you may have ADD.

COMPONENTS OF A THOROUGH ADD TEST REPORT

A good evaluation looks at you as a whole individual. It should not only address the issue of ADD, but also take a much broader look at how you are feeling and functioning.

In the hands of a skilled adult ADD diagnostician, the results of an evaluation of adult ADD and related issues should provide a detailed blueprint for treatment. This treatment plan should suggest the types of treatment that may prove most useful, detail the issues needing to be addressed in treatment, and suggest a range of educational material and compensatory strategies for the adult with ADD.

As an informed consumer, you should expect far more than a simple "yes-no" response to the question of an ADD diagnosis. A thorough test report should include:

- A summary of your history, with a focus on ADD issues, as well as a focus on any other medical/psychological issues that may be suggested in that history

- A list of all tests administered, with scores and an interpretation of those scores

- A summary of findings

- A diagnosis (This section should also address whether the examiner believes that there may be issues of concern in addition to or other than ADD.)

- A list of recommendations including:

  1. Whether further testing is indicated

  2. Whether referral for treatment by other professionals is indicated

  3. Whether an evaluation for medication is indicated

  4. Issues of concern to be focused on in counseling or psychotherapy

MEDICAL TESTS FOR ADD

Currently there are no medical tests for ADD that are commonly used and recognized as diagnostic tools. There are, however, medical tests that may show differences between ADD and non-ADD individuals. For example, PET (Positron Emission Tomography) scans, which measure glucose metabolism in the brain, were used by Dr. Alan Zametkin in his research on differences between ADD and non-ADD brains. (See Chapter 1.) Research continues at the National Institute of Mental Health using PET scans.

Some work has been done using SPECT (Single Photon Emission Computerized Tomography) scans as a diagnostic tool to evaluate ADD; however, these techniques are not widely used or recognized by the general medical community at this time.

There is also some evidence of different brain-wave patterns in response to brief visual stimuli, as measured by EEGs in adults with ADD as opposed to those without ADD. Although some claim that EEGs can be used diagnostically, the general consensus among professionals in the field does not support this view.

As a medical consumer, however, you should be aware that none of these tests has been accepted as a diagnostic tool at this time.

ARE THERE DIFFERENT TYPES OF ADD?

As noted in Chapter 1, the three officially recognized subtypes of ADD, as described in the DSM-IV, are the:

1. Predominantly hyperactive-impulsive type

2. Predominantly inattentive type

3. Combined type

There is not universal agreement, however, about these subtypes. For example, Dr. Russell Barkley, an internationally known figure in the field of ADD, now hypothesizes that ADD with hyperactivity is a disorder completely unrelated to ADD without hyperactivity.

Others in the ADD field propose a number of subtypes of ADD, although these have not been thoroughly understood or documented. Some speculate that different subtypes of ADD may respond best to different combinations of medications. Others propose that we are currently lumping a number of different neurochemical disorders under the common name of ADD, and that, as we gain more understanding, we will gradually delineate a number of different, but related disorders.

WHAT CONDITIONS COMMONLY COEXIST WITH ADD?

Depression

Depression very commonly coexists with ADD in adulthood. Researchers find that rates of both anxiety and depression are higher among relatives of those with ADD than in the general population. There is speculation about a possible link between ADD and depression. Newly diagnosed adults with ADD with a prior psychiatric history were most often diagnosed with depression.

Anxiety

Like depression, anxiety is commonly found among adults with ADD. Adults with ADD tend to be very reactive to stress in general and to become anxious when stressed. Learning to create a low-stress lifestyle is an important aspect of learning to live successfully with ADD. (More about this in our discussion of coping skills in Chapter 4.) Some adults with ADD have tremendous difficulty in controlling their anger, and other ADD adults may exhibit extreme overreactions and outbursts that are really expressions of stress and anxiety. Many women with ADD report that their anxiety levels are most elevated during their premenstrual period.

Learning Disabilities

There are strong links between ADD and LD. It is possible for a person to have ADD without any learning disabilities, although some experts in the field believe that other neurodevelopmental problems always coexist with ADD. The links may be obvious when learning disabilities are significant, or they may be more subtle in nature.

ADD is a condition that is responsive to medication, whereas learning disabilities are generally considered to be due to structural differences in the brain that cannot be treated by medication.

Adults with ADD should be evaluated and treated by a professional who has enough knowledge about learning disabilities to make an appropriate referral for evaluation if appropriate. Learning disabilities are treated by tutoring and by learning strategies to compensate for areas of difficulty. With the growing recognition of both ADD and LD in adults that were not identified earlier, more tutors are working with adults.

Tutoring may be a very important part of treatment for ADD/LD problems. This is especially true if the ADD adult works in a field that requires continued training and education or desires to pursue further education. Tutoring can have a specific focus, such as to improve writing skills, or it can be more general, emphasizing study skills, time management, and organizational skills for returning students who may have been deficient in these skills in their earlier student days. Many adults with ADD experience difficulty writing because they are unable to organize their thoughts coherently and have difficulty deciding what information to include and what to omit. A tutor can be very helpful in learning these skills.

Educational specialists can also be helpful to adults with ADD by introducing them to various types of assistive technologies, such as voice recognition software for individuals who have difficulty with written expression.

Substance Abuse

There is also a strong link between ADD and substance abuse for some, but not all, individuals with ADD. Adolescents with ADD who are hyperactive, impulsive, and show some degree of conduct disorder are statistically much more likely to develop patterns of substance abuse than are adolescents with the primarily inattentive subtype of ADD.

In the past there has been much difficulty in obtaining appropriate, coordinated treatment for both conditions simultaneously. Those who treat substance abusers adhere to a philosophy of avoiding medication in treatment. Some physicians fear that stimulant medications prescribed for ADD may be potentially abused by ADD substance abusers.

Very recently, however, research on ways to treat ADD substance abusers has shown that stimulant medication helps control impulsive behavior. Contrary to fears among some in the field of substance abuse, professionals in the ADD field are now finding that it can be helpful to prescribe stimulant medication to ADD substance abusers to assist them in avoiding a relapse. More research needs to be done on this important topic, and current information about treating ADD substance abuse needs to be disseminated to the medical community.

Obsessive-Compulsive Disorder

OCD (Obsessive-Compulsive Disorder) may also share some sort of link, possibly genetic, with ADD. Some research groups find a high incidence of OCD among adults with ADD, whereas other research groups have not found this strong connection between the two disorders.

ADD adults with OCD may report that they are highly perfectionistic about many things and find it impossible to prioritize because they feel compelled to do everything to perfection. ("All my to-do items are A's!") They may report that they are unable to accomplish all that they need to do because they become obsessively involved in one project and are unable to pull themselves away to focus on other things. They may report that they have tremendous difficulty in throwing things away and may display patterns of collecting things. Often their lives reflect uncontrolled chaos as they obsessively, but ineffectively, pursue perfection.

Neurological Disorders

ADD symptoms are also symptomatic of neurological disorders that may be the result of head injury, exposure to toxins such as lead, or to diseases such as encephalitis. Similarly, ADD symptoms may be observed resulting from birth trauma, oxygen deprivation at birth, or prematurity. If a person relates strong patterns of ADD symptoms, but reports no history of ADD symptoms among close relatives, the clinician should look carefully at other possible medical causes. Neurological screening should be a routine part of every ADD evaluation in order to make an appropriate neurological referral if indicated.

Other Conditions

There are numerous other disorders in which ADD-like symptoms may be displayed. Some of these include:

Mania
Excessive use of caffeine
Periods of high stress and anxiety
Impulse disorders
Chronic fatigue
Hyper- or hypothyroidism
Personality disorders
Tourette's Syndrome

Because so many disorders can mimic ADD, a thorough evaluation is critical. Even in the hands of a professional who is familiar with ADD in adults, it is possible to make a misdiagnosis.

DECIDING WHETHER TESTING IS APPROPRIATE

In some instances you will need test documentation of your ADD. This is most likely to be true if you are returning to school and need documentation of ADD in order to qualify for educational supports and accommodations. If you are engaged in negotiations with your employer in which you are requesting accommodations at work, your employer may ask for more documentation than a simple statement from a physician that you have ADD.

Some people feel much more comfortable being tested for ADD because they are unsure of the diagnosis and don't want to be casually, and perhaps incorrectly, diagnosed. In other cases, during the clinical interview it may become apparent that several related conditions are involved. More complicated issues of differential diagnosis and diagnosis of coexisting conditions may require a more thorough and painstaking evaluation process, including testing.

A general rule of thumb is that the less experience a professional has in working with adults with ADD, the more helpful it may be to obtain a complete test battery. Similarly, the more complex your history of treatment, and the more varied your symptoms, the more helpful a full test battery may be.

3

Treating Adult ADD: Medication and Psychotherapy

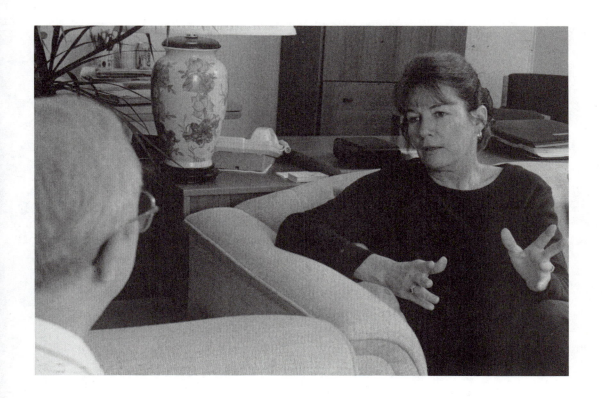

Treating Adult ADD: Medication and Psychotherapy

How Is ADD Treated?

ADD is not a "psychological" disorder, although people with ADD may have coexisting psychological disorders such as anxiety or depression. ADD is a neurobiological disorder, often accompanied by psychological issues. Psychological disorders such as low self-esteem and depression often result from years of struggling with ADD issues without help and without understanding the basis of these problems. ADD cannot be treated effectively if it is approached by a psychotherapist in a traditional insight-oriented, nondirective fashion. Such an approach can be helpful for individuals with ADD, but it is not effective as treatment for the core ADD symptoms. Effective treatment of ADD needs to be multimodal, utilizing medication, education, psychotherapy, cognitive retraining approaches, coaching, and sometimes auxiliary therapies such as tutoring, career counseling, and speech therapy. You will find more detailed information about each of these approaches throughout this chapter.

MEDICATION

Stimulant Medication

First, let's look at some common misunderstandings. Many people, even professionals, are not yet familiar with treating ADD in adults by using the same types of stimulant medications that have proven effective in treating children and adolescents.

For years it was believed that stimulants had a "paradoxical" effect on children, calming them down instead of stimulating them. This myth of paradoxical effect persists today, leading many people to presume that adults cannot be treated with stimulants.

On the contrary, adults are being treated very effectively with stimulant medication. We now understand that stimulant medication works, for both children and adults, by making more dopamine and norepenephrine available for use by the frontal lobes. This increase in available neurotransmitters allows our brains to exert better control, to monitor our actions and reactions more effectively, to decrease impulsivity, and to increase our ability to focus effectively.

Stimulants Used to Treat ADD in Adults

- Ritalin (methylphenidate)

- Dexedrine (dextroamphetamine)

- Cylert (pemoline)

- Desoxyn (methamphetamine)

- Adderol (previously called Obetrol, a combination of different stimulant medications)

Adderol, initially marketed under the name Obetrol for obesity control, has been found to be very useful in treating some adults for ADD symptoms. Clinical trials are currently underway as part of the process of receiving approval for its use in the treatment of ADD. Until it receives such approval, it can only be prescribed by physicians who elect to participate in those clinical trials.

Side effects of stimulant medication can include:

- Insomnia

- Decreased appetite

- Weight loss

- Headaches

- Increased heart rate/ blood pressure

- Rebound effect as dose "wears off"

- Motor tics

Some adults experience negative side effects from one stimulant, but none when taking another. Also, some adults seem to benefit more from one psychostimulant than another. The positive benefits of stimulant medication can sometimes decrease over time. Recent research suggests that adults typically benefit from higher doses of stimulant medication than do children, and that "non-responders" to stimulant medication may simply need higher doses in order for it to be effective.

Is Stimulant Medication Effective?

Many individuals have reported that they are not sure what to look for when taking stimulant medication. Not all adults experience the same benefits from stimulants. Here are some of the benefits reported by adults with ADD when taking stimulants:

- "Foggy feeling" goes away

- Able to concentrate for longer periods

- Able to read with focus

- Less distracted

- Able to refocus on a task after an interruption

- Able to "think things through" more thoroughly

- Less mental fatigue

- More energy, especially later in the day

- Less forgetful

Antidepressants

In addition to the use of stimulants, there are a number of newer antidepressant medications that have been used very effectively in combination with a stimulant. Often such a combined medication approach is more effective than stimulants alone. Antidepressants metabolize more slowly in the body, which means that there is a more steady flow of medication. By contrast, stimulants metabolize very rapidly. Some adults experience very uneven effects throughout the day as their stimulant medication peaks in effectiveness and then rapidly declines. The combination of an antidepressant with a stimulant tends to reduce these "peaks and valleys" throughout the day. Secondly, many adults with ADD report feeling somewhat anxious or jittery when taking only stimulant medication. A combined medication approach seems to ameliorate these feelings. Adults who are prone to anxiety may experience increased feelings of anxiety when taking a stimulant alone but do well on a combination of antidepressant and stimulant.

Some of the antidepressants that are prescribed in combination with stimulants include:

Brand Name	Generic Name
Prozac	Fluoxetine
Zoloft	Sertraline
Paxil	Paroxetine
Wellbutrin	Bupropion
Norpramin	Desipramine
Tofranil	Imipramine

These medications belong to different families of drugs and are effective in different ways. It is very important, for this reason, that a psychiatrist, neurologist, or psychopharmacologist who is highly experienced in treating the array of symptoms related to ADD be consulted to prescribe these medications.

Medications for Related Disorders

A range of symptoms may be associated with ADD in adults. Many adults with ADD are treated simultaneously for these related disorders, including:

Obsessive-Compulsive Disorder

For obsessive-compulsive symptoms, such as obsessional thinking, compulsive repetitive behaviors, hoarding, or extreme perfectionism, one of several medications may be useful:

Brand Name	Generic Name
Anafranil	clomipramine
Prozac	fluoxetine
Zoloft	sertraline

Tantrums, Rage Reactions, or Violence

Some adults experience extreme anger reactions, completely out of proportion to the event precipitating the response. This can range from yelling and door slamming to out-of-control physical violence. Several medications have been found useful to diminish such rage reactions. They include:

Brand Name	Generic Name
(generally called by its generic name)	Lithium
Tegretol	Carbamazepine
Depakote	Divalproex

Tension, Jitteriness

Some adults with ADD experience extreme physical tension or feelings of jitteriness. For some, this is a side effect of taking stimulant medication. For others, it is an internal state symptomatic of their ADD. For both groups, however, certain medications may be helpful. They include the beta-blockers:

Brand Name	Generic Name
Inderol	propranolol
Corgard	nadolol

PSYCHOTHERAPY

Although there has been little opportunity for research on this subject, a consensus seems to have developed, in clinics and among clinicians who treat adults with ADD, concerning the most helpful treatment approaches. Clinical experience tells us that the most helpful approaches for treating adults with ADD share the following characteristics:

- **Practical.** Aimed at coping with problems of daily living

- **Focused.** Addresses specific issues rather than wandering randomly from topic to topic

- **Directive.** Therapist offers direct, practical advice and suggests approaches

- **Solution-oriented.** Focused on results without ignoring feelings

- **Educational.** Increases understanding of ADD and its effects

- **Supportive.** Provides understanding and encouragement

- **Insight coupled with action.** Insight into patterns or problems always linked to specific actions aimed at solving problems

Therapy that is most helpful for adults with ADD needs to be multifaceted. Typically, adults with ADD need to deal with a number of issues that may include interpersonal issues, problems with self-esteem and self-image, as well as practical problems involving career, education, and daily living. Goals and priorities need to be set with your therapist's help. You may decide to engage in different types of therapy or obtain various forms of assistance at different times in your treatment, depending on the priorities you establish.

Group Psychotherapy

Adult ADD group psychotherapy may be extremely useful because it provides the opportunity to talk with other adults who are struggling with the same issues. Being around other ADD adults may provide you with the support you need to learn to accept yourself and to learn techniques for managing and minimizing troublesome ADD symptoms. A psychotherapy group for adults with ADD is quite different from a support group and is designed for different purposes, although both groups may be very useful as components of your treatment for ADD. Typically a psychotherapy group is led by a psychotherapist who is expert in adult ADD. It is much smaller than many support groups—usually six to twelve people who meet together weekly. Psychotherapy groups are confidential and are designed to allow individuals to come to know one another in a very personal fashion and to work with one another on very intimate, difficult issues.

Psychotherapy groups for adults with ADD may sometimes be structured.

Just as it can be most helpful for individual psychotherapy with ADD adults to be structured, the same can hold true for group psychotherapy. In such cases, the group may decide to focus on a single topic or issue for a period of time, with each group member reporting weekly on his or her progress in tackling the problem the group is working on.

Couples Therapy

Bringing a partner of an adult with ADD into the treatment process can be very beneficial for both parties. The observations and feedback of the partner can provide very useful information to the therapist. Typically, many adults with ADD are not accurate self-observers, nor are they accurate observers of their impact on those around them. Often the input of a spouse can be essential in helping the adult with ADD become aware of problematic patterns and, more surprisingly, even to become aware of positive changes. For example, on occasion an adult with ADD will report that he or she sees little if any benefit from medication, while his or her spouse, on the other hand, reports marked positive changes.

Aside from playing the role of observer and reporter, the involvement of the spouse can be essential to the success of treatment for a number of reasons. First, the spouse of an adult with ADD often has been playing an exhausting role for years. Often the lion's share of responsibility for organizing and managing the household falls upon the non-ADD spouse. This inequity can lead to resentment, anger, and blame.

The spouse needs support, understanding, and education about how ADD affects his or her partner. The couple needs to work together to make joint life decisions that can better accommodate the spouse with ADD while taking the needs of the non-ADD spouse into account as well.

The area of spousal relations is so critical to the successful treatment of a married adult with ADD that an entire chapter has been devoted to marital issues. (See Chapter 5.)

"Traditional" Psychotherapy

Unfortunately, many adults with ADD report that they have been in therapy, sometimes more than once, but have not gained much benefit in dealing with their ADD symptoms. Therapy can be helpful to adults with ADD, but it is essential that the therapist understand ADD and how to be most helpful to adults with ADD.

Sometimes, though, therapy is not helpful and can even be destructive. For example, a therapist familiar with ADD may place psychological interpretations on ADD symptoms such as chronic lateness, forgetfulness, and poor follow-through. Although there may be a psychological component to some of these patterns, it is critical that both therapist and client understand that such patterns in ADD adults have a neurochemical basis and need to be addressed with practical techniques rather than interpreted as a "psychological" issue. Some adults report that they have struggled with frustration and low self-esteem for years because they tried, with their therapist's guidance, to understand the "passive-aggressive" motivations behind forgetting an important anniversary or behind patterns of chronic lateness. Rather than engaging in more self-doubt and self-blame, adults with ADD need to learn tools to manage and minimize such troublesome patterns.

Another reason that more traditional psychotherapy may not be useful is that it tends to be unstructured and free-flowing. While such techniques may be useful for adults who are working to unmask hidden feelings and motivations, unstructured psychotherapy sessions are often ineffective for adults with ADD. ADD adults are already too unstructured in their thought patterns and living patterns. When psychotherapy is unstructured, the adult with ADD tends to wander unproductively from one topic to the next and may typically have little memory of what has taken place in the session once it has ended.

Adults with ADD often need structuring aids and reminders to keep on track in therapy. Such aids might include:

- Keeping a notebook during the week to jot down thoughts, questions, and problems to bring up during the next session

- Being assigned specific "homework" to work on between sessions

- Taking notes during the session of key points, goals, and issues

- Receiving a brief "wrap-up" at the end of each session to reemphasize key issues that were discussed and as a reminder of goals to work on during the week

- Refocusing the session if the client has distracted himself with some tangential topic

More Information About Treating Adults with ADD

The list of resources for psychotherapists who treat adults with ADD is beginning to grow substantially. It may be useful to refer your therapist to the Resource List provided at the back of the book.

Therapists who want to become more active in treating adults with ADD should join national organizations such as CH.A.D.D. and ADDA and attend their annual meetings and conventions. Both CH.A.D.D. and ADDA provide many seminars on adult ADD issues at their annual meetings each year. For therapists who are unable to attend these meetings, it is possible to order tapes of all these sessions. The addresses for ordering such tapes are included in the Resource List.

It is also very important to receive more direct training in the diagnosis and treatment of adults with ADD. Some brief workshops on adult ADD have been offered for the past few years in conjunction with longer training sessions dealing with childhood ADD issues. Workshops exclusively focused on adult ADD are beginning to be offered.

If there is a professional in your community or in an accessible community nearby who is an expert in adult ADD, it may be useful to arrange for periodic training or consultation on adult ADD treatment issues.

OTHER USEFUL TREATMENT APPROACHES

Support Groups for ADD Adults

More and more of these groups are developing in communities all over the United States. Lists of existing groups can be obtained through contacting the national organizations listed in the Resource List. If your community does not have a support group, why not think about helping to start one?

Support groups can be quite varied. Some are small informal groups that meet in the homes of participants. Such groups provide a very valuable opportunity for self-expression among people who will understand your struggles with ADD. They also provide the opportunity to learn of the ADD struggles of others and to provide mutual support and suggestions. There is often a large collective wisdom about ADD issues within a group of ADD adults that can be an invaluable source of help as you learn to manage your own ADD.

Other support groups are larger, more structured, and more informative or educational in nature. Such groups may meet in a church or school on a monthly basis, with structured programs, speakers, and educational materials available.

Both types of support groups can be very useful, each in its own way, but neither type of support group should be considered to be a substitute for therapy. See also the section on support groups in Chapter 11.

Education About Adult ADD

Just as your therapist needs to know about adult ADD, you too need to become an expert on adult ADD. Not all adults with ADD are alike. You need to know about your own unique set of strengths and weaknesses and to learn which patterns can be changed, which need to be accommodated, and ways you can learn to compensate for problems caused by ADD.

If reading is hard for you, which is true for many adults with ADD, you may prefer to listen to audiotapes and/or to watch videotapes dealing with adult ADD subjects. Names and addresses of organizations from which you can order these tapes are provided in the Resource List. Attending an adult ADD support group that provides information about adult ADD also can be an important tool in your process of self-education.

ADD is a condition you need to take charge of. Knowledge is the first step toward taking charge. Through reading, listening, and talking, you can begin to learn techniques and strategies that have been helpful for others who share some of the same problems in their daily lives.

Career Counseling

Career and workplace issues are such important topics for most adults with ADD that we have devoted an entire section of this book to job-related concerns. It is important to mention career issues here, too, because they are so often neglected in ADD treatment plans. Some work-related issues may be entirely appropriate to focus on in your ongoing individual psychotherapy. These issues may involve difficulties with supervisors or co-workers. Your therapist may also be able to assist you in developing strategies to be on time and better organized at work. If your problems at work are severe, you may need to work with someone who has more direct experience in ADD workplace issues. This may be true if you feel you are at risk to lose your job; if you need accommodations at work and have not been able to obtain them; or if you feel you need to change career directions. For a more complete discussion of these issues, turn to Chapter 8.

ADD Coaching

Follow-through is one of the biggest challenges in learning to manage ADD symptoms. You may finish reading an article, attend a seminar, or leave your therapist's office full of resolve to build a new habit or try a new coping skill, only to find that after trying once or twice you fall back into old patterns. It is difficult for all of us to break old habits or to build new ones, but it is especially difficult when you have ADD. Adults with ADD not only have to struggle, as we all do, with the difficult task of self-discipline, but also must struggle with forgetfulness, distractibility, impulse control, and a host of other issues that may interfere with the new desired behavior.

If you find that this is the case for you, you may need to have a "coach." Just as in sports, an ADD coach is someone who is there to encourage you, to inspire you, to remind you, or to report to. And just as coaching is highly beneficial in developing athletic skills, ADD coaching can be essential in developing the new coping skills you need to improve the quality of your life.

A good coach is:

- Encouraging

- Supportive

- Consistent

- Available

- Calm

- Non-"nagging"

A National Coaching Network has been established and is expanding to serve the needs of adults with ADD. (See the Resource List for information about contacting this network.) ADD coaches are professionals who can work with ADD adults on a regular, even daily basis, for short periods of time, to provide encouragement, structure, focus, and a reminder of short-term goals.

Some therapists who work with ADD adults establish a daily "check-in" on the therapist's "coach-line." This check-in works as follows: The therapist may see his or her client once a week in order to establish goals for the upcoming week. The client then agrees to "check in" daily with the therapist, by leaving a brief message on the therapist's answering machine that tells him or her what the client has (or has not) accomplished that day.

Some adults have established relationships with other ADD adults whereby they check in with each other daily in order to help keep each other on track. The primary risk in such a relationship is that the daily "check-in" becomes a prolonged distraction from accomplishing the tasks of the day!

ADD Tutoring

More and more tutors are beginning to work with adults as well as with children, as they have done traditionally in the past. Tutors who specialize in working with individuals who have ADD typically are very proficient at teaching organizational skills.

Most ADD-experienced tutors can help you organize a long-term, complex project, and then can monitor you as you bring that task to completion.

Tutors are also skilled at teaching organizational techniques relating to writing. Adults with ADD may tend to ramble, to be tangential, and to lose focus as they write. Many adults with ADD report that they have tremendous difficulty discerning what information is essential and what is nonessential when they attempt to write or study. Adults with ADD who are returning to school, or who need to do a significant amount of writing on their job, can benefit from working with a tutor to enhance their organizational skills.

Professional Organizers

As life becomes more complex, and as all of our lives seem to become busier, the need for organization increases. There is now a National Association of Professional Organizers, whose growing ranks attest to the challenge that all of us, even those without ADD, face in working to keep ourselves and our belongings orderly.

For people with ADD, the occasional help of a professional organizer can make the difference between order and chaos. The biggest struggle for many adults with ADD, however, is to give themselves permission to ask for help. Unfortunately, some adults with ADD only blame and criticize themselves for their disorganization. They tell themselves that they "shouldn't" need a professional's help in organizing. Getting beyond "should" or "shouldn't" to a practical, matter-of-fact attitude about strengths and weaknesses is perhaps the biggest step an adult with ADD can take toward learning to manage this disability.

A professional organizer typically makes on-site visits to your home or office and assists you in a hands-on fashion to organize your desk, your paperwork, your closet, your kitchen, or even your household. Typically organizers charge by the hour and are able to accomplish a great deal in a short amount of time— after all, they are professional organizers! Often they are called in to help when paperwork becomes overwhelming. They can help to efficiently decide which papers are to be kept and which to discard. They are expert in helping to establish efficient, workable filing systems and in helping you decide which papers you need to be able to access instantly and which can be placed in longer-term files.

Organizers can also make recommendations about the size and type of storage system, shelves, and files in order to maintain order once it has been established. Some professional organizers have regular contracts, returning every three months, or every six months, to help reestablish order.

Time-Management Seminars

There are numerous time-management seminars that typically market their services to the business community. Time wasting and inefficiency are very expensive in the business world, and corporations are increasingly willing to pay the cost for their employees to attend seminars designed to make them more effective and productive. These seminars are often focused on learning to use a day-planning system as a structuring device for managing time.

These seminars can be highly useful but often hold drawbacks for adults with ADD. The first drawback is that such seminars typically extend over six or seven hours, long past the time span during which an adult with ADD can concentrate. Secondly, these seminars are "one-shot deals." You sign up for the seminar, listen to the lecture, and go home full of resolve. Of course, the hard work begins the next day—putting the plan into action. Many adults with ADD report that they have tried almost every organizational tool in the world, and, just like the chronic dieter, they find themselves back to their old tricks within a few days or weeks.

These initial seminars need to be backed up with follow-through. Some seminars sell tapes that can be reviewed repeatedly as "booster shots." It can also be helpful to use a coach or therapist to reinforce building new habits based on the time-management system.

DEVELOPING A PROGRAM OF TREATMENT

If you are fortunate, you will find a therapist who is skilled and experienced in working with ADD adults. This therapist cannot, necessarily, provide you with all the pieces of the puzzle but will hopefully serve as a coordinator of services and as someone who can refer you to appropriate resources.

If your therapist is not highly experienced in working with adults with ADD, you may need to advocate for yourself and to actively seek the resources and assistance that you need.

If there is an adult support group in your area, join it. They generally are excellent sources of information about the professionals in the community who are expert in working with adults with ADD. If there is no support group, consider starting one! (See Chapter 11 for more on this.)

Another good source for information and resources are books on adult ADD. Most, if not all of them, provide lists of organizations and resources.

As you work with your therapist to put together the pieces of the treatment puzzle, remember, as much as you would like to, you can't "fix" everything at once. You will need, with the help of your therapist, to set priorities. Adult ADDers often try to tackle everything at once and end by feeling overwhelmed and ineffective. Start with the most critical area of your life, develop coping strategies, and make life changes in that area. Then move on to the next. That way, each success is built on the stable support of the previous accomplishment. Take it slow and remember: success breeds success!

4

Learning Life-Management Skills

Learning Life-Management Skills

AM I THE ONLY ONE IN SUCH CHAOS?

Absolutely not! No matter what state of chaos your closet, your checkbook, your desk, or your entire house is in, you've got plenty of company. An adult ADD support group sponsored an evening program entitled "Coming Out of the ADD Closet—If I Can Find the Door." For fun, they invited group members to bring photographs of their chaos, awarding a prize to the "biggest mess." While it's reassuring to know that others experience the same difficulty in organizing their lives, sometimes the level of disorganization in which ADD adults live is no laughing matter. This chapter is focused on learning skills to reduce and contain the chaos.

HOW CAN I LEARN TO MANAGE MY ADD?

This section will provide you with a large set of tools to develop life-management skills. Don't make the mistake of expecting too much of yourself too soon.

Many adults with ADD report that they have made repeated resolutions to "get organized" or to "get control of finances" only to find that a week or month later they are back in their old patterns, feeling defeated. In order to be successful in managing your ADD over the long term, you need to do some rethinking about how life changes are achieved.

Become an *Actor* Instead of a *Reactor*

Many persons with ADD are trapped in a reactive mode. Reactors may appear to be active, or even hyperactive, as they respond to their environment. In a different sense, though, reactors are very passive. They wait for the environment to stimulate them, to give them cues, merely responding to whatever random events come their way. Reactors rely on chance, mood, or happenstance to set the course.

An "actor" is someone who acts deliberately, who sets an agenda, and who acts on the environment, rather than just reacting to it. An actor seeks to direct and control his world. He is a problem solver, a solution finder. An actor works to develop better ways of responding to the environment, actively seeking to create a supportive environment.

If you make only one change in yourself to better manage your ADD, the most important change you can make is to learn to think and behave as an actor. As an actor you will discover ways to work with your ADD rather than letting your ADD work against you.

Learn How to Develop Habits

Some fortunate people learn how to build habits when they are children. They learn those skills through growing up in a predictable environment in which parents and teachers support the development of toothbrushing, bed making, homework completion, and the like. Children learn habit and skill development from piano teachers, coaches, and parents.

For many children with ADD, however, their neurochemical difficulties may have interfered with learning how to develop skills and habits. Without the benefit of treatment for their ADD in childhood, many adults report that they have never developed the self-discipline and persistence necessary to build habits.

Using an ADD Coach to Develop New Habits

Just as children need the guidance of parents, teachers, tutors, and coaches, adults with ADD can benefit greatly from structured guidance as they work toward habit development. Don't let false pride get in the way of seeking support while you develop the life-management skills you need. Breaking old habits and forming new ones is hard work for anyone and is doubly hard work for adults with ADD.

Because adults with ADD often experience enormous difficulty in their efforts to make lasting changes in behavior patterns, a new profession is emerging—ADD coaching. (See the section on ADD coaching in Chapter 3.)

ADD coaches may come from a variety of backgrounds—education, psychology, social work, counseling, to name a few—and serve as persons who can provide advice and structure as well as assist with goal setting and follow-through. Unlike psychotherapy, contact with an ADD coach is focused on the practical aspects of daily functioning. Contact with coaches is typically brief and frequent, sometimes daily. Coaching can take place face-to-face, by phone, and by E–mail. To find a trained ADD coach, you can contact the National Coaching Network. (See the Resource List.)

Don't Treat New Habits Like a Crash Diet

Many adults with ADD have made statements such as "I've tried to get organized a hundred times, but it never lasts." "I've bought half a dozen day planners over the years, but I've never used them for long." These adults, typically, have approached life-management techniques like a crash diet. Full of resolve, they clear off the desk, clean out the closet, or purchase the day planner. A few days later they find they are right back to their old tricks.

Learning life-management skills is the process of developing many, many small patterns or habits. For a resolution to become a habit, it needs to be repeated many times. Finally, when a pattern becomes habitual, after many repetitions, it will no longer require much effort. Many well-intentioned adults with ADD start off by making great efforts, efforts that are too ambitious to sustain, just like a crash diet. They are never able to reach the point of payoff, when it's no longer hard work to maintain the desired behavior. Breaking down a task into tiny, do-able bits is often the key to successful habit building.

HABIT BUILDING WITH A DAY PLANNER

A "day planner" is a notebook that provides space to write a "to do" list and/or schedule for each day. There are several well-known brands including Day Runner and the Franklin Planner. Although a day planner can be a very useful tool for adults with ADD, many ADD adults report that they have never successfully developed the habit of using one.

Successful use of a day planner involves multiple steps. If we take the approach of breaking a task down into do-able bits, an adult with ADD who decides to start using a day planner might do well to set one simple goal: to learn to carry the day planner with him/her at all times, whether or not it is used effectively. Think about that goal for a minute. What might get in the way of building that habit, and what are some possible solutions?

1. Think of what type of day planner you are most likely to keep with you.

    - Would a day planner that comes with a shoulder strap be less likely to be left behind?

    - Are you more likely to use a day planner that is small enough to slip in a pocket?

    - Would a brightly colored cover make your day planner less likely to be lost or forgotten?

    - Would you make better use of a computerized day planner?

2. Develop a single, accessible place to keep your day planner, both at home and at work. Often a good place is near a telephone. That way you'll have it by your side to refer to and to write in as you talk on the phone.

3. Keep a note by the front door or in your car if you are prone to walk out of the house or the office without your day planner.

4. Make one simple resolution, which you will keep for a month, to go back to your house or office to retrieve your day planner, if you find you have rushed out without it.

Once you have developed the habit of always carrying your day planner, the next step is to build the habit of referring to it at regular times—for example, when arriving at work in the morning and when leaving the office at the end of the day. When those habits are established, you can begin to fine-tune habits of how and where to make notations and reminders, how to use it as a goal-setting tool, or how to customize it for your own particular needs. Once you have developed the habit of keeping your day planner with you as a constant companion, it can become a powerful tool to assist in organization, prioritization, goal setting, and time management. (The same kind of step-by-step approach can be used to work on building better health habits or toward developing a better relationship with your spouse.)

Developing a Blueprint

For adults whose lives have any degree of complexity, and that includes most of us, learning to use a day planner is essential for good time management. Day planners should contain much more than a simple list of daily appointments. A daily page in a day planner should be considered a blueprint for your day. The day planner itself should be used to develop the blueprint for your year. Some planners even contain pages for longer-term planning. When you make the best use of a day planner, you are using it as a system to help you think about your goals and values, both short-term and long-term. The day planner should then be used to turn those goals into concrete events and tasks.

Daily Planning Sessions

Some adults with ADD report that even when they write things in their day planner, they forget to look at it. Either they became distracted by the events of their day or they "were sure" they remembered what they had written and so felt no need to check! A habit of daily planning sessions needs to be built into your day. Some adults find it better to routinely check their day planner twice a day for a planning session: first, as they begin their day at the office; then, second, as they prepare to leave their office for the day. This second session allows them to shift gears from workplace goals and events to private life.

Include Your Whole Day, Not Just Your Workday

To serve as a memory aid and to help you set goals in your life, all of your day's events and plans should be included. Write in your schedule the hour you plan to exercise. Include time in the evening to talk with your spouse, spend time with friends, take a course, or whatever other personal goals you may have.

TIME-MANAGEMENT TECHNIQUES

Good time management requires a number of skills that are typically difficult for adults with ADD. Managing our time well requires:

Planning
Prioritization
Memory
Accurate assessment of time requirements
Mid-course corrections due to unexpected events
Ability to resist appealing distractions in order to stick with the plan
Ability to keep track of the passage of time while engaged in activities
Ability to shift smoothly from one activity to the next during the day

Time Management Is Life Management

Although you may not think of it in this way, time management is synonymous with life management. Time is simply the way we divide up our lives into measurable segments. All too often, people think of time management as a technique for getting lots of undesirable chores or tasks accomplished. Although we all have undesirable but necessary chores in our lives, good time management is not the business of checking items off a bothersome "to do" list. Good time management means that we step back from our lives far enough to gain perspective and to use that perspective to make decisions about how we will use our lives (and therefore our time). This process of taking stock should be a regularly occurring event. As our lives evolve, as jobs change, as we marry, raise children, and as children grow up and leave home, our goals and priorities will change many times. Good time management takes those changes into account.

Good time management requires being an "actor" rather than a "reactor" with regard to life events. Good time management also requires that we learn to monitor ourselves as we go through our day. "Am I on track?" "Am I accomplishing those things that are most important to me?" "Have I allowed the events of the day, or the demands of others, to take precedence over my own goals for today?" This is not to suggest that you should set a plan for the day and then follow it rigidly. You are in charge of your time. If events change, or even if your mood or inclination changes, you certainly have the right to change your plans and priorities for the day. Many ADDers have so much difficulty charting a course for their day, however, that they feel lost until the random events of the day, and the people with whom they have contact during the day, set their course for them.

Avoiding Time-Management Pitfalls

After you have developed a habitual daily planning session and a surer sense of your goals and priorities, there are still a number of tendencies, common to most adults with ADD, that you will need to recognize and guard against as you go through your day. Here are some of the most likely time-management wreckers:

Overbooking

Many adults with ADD tend to repeatedly underestimate how long tasks will take. They don't tend to do contingency planning—for weather, traffic, or late starts, for example. Nor do they take into account their own distractibility and how that may slow them down. As a result, whether at work or during leisure, they find themselves feeling rushed and being late. People who chronically overbook themselves don't allow time for thoughtful, careful work. Some people, unconsciously, may even use this technique as a self-defense against compulsive perfectionism or from a fear of inadequacy. They think, "If I wait until the last minute and am rushed, then no one, including myself, can expect me to do a perfect job." More often, however, the overbooking is simply a function of unrealistic planning.

 Solution: Experiment with "underbooking" yourself. Look at the events in your day planner for the previous day. How many tasks and scheduled events were crammed into your day? Consciously try to cut down on that number. Monitor your stress level. Experiment with arriving at each destination even five minutes early.

Out-of-Control "To Do" Lists

One thing ADDers are really good at is thinking up new ideas! They tend to be masters of adding items to a never-ending "to do" list, but not so good at paring those lists down to a "do-able" length. New time management computer programs are generally designed to automatically move forward, to the next day, week, or month any tasks that are not checked off as completed. Many adults with ADD, who use such programs, find that their daily task list is always grow-ing, out of control, and too large for the space provided for it on the computer screen. If you have a rolling and growing list of 30 or 40 "to do" items, it becomes much harder to operate efficiently. Often you may be tempted to tackle the easy, short tasks just for the sake of visibly shortening the list, while leaving the more complicated, but critical, tasks undone.

Solution: Experiment with your daily task list. Review your progress at the end of each day. Pare your list down again and again until you are consis-tently completing the tasks listed by the day's end. If you complete your list and have more time and energy, there is nothing to prevent you from tackling a few items from tomorrow's task list!

Consider yourself a success when you have shortened your list to the point that you are consistently completing it each day.

Procrastination

Procrastination is often one of the biggest schedule breakers of them all. Many adults with ADD report that they have struggled all their lives with a strong ten-dency to procrastinate. While there is no "sure cure" for procrastination, there are a number of things you can do that may reduce its negative impact on your life.

Why do you procrastinate? A brief, not very illuminating answer to that question is: "Because I don't feel like doing something." It may help to look beyond that to understand why.

Have you organized your life so that it is filled with requirements you dislike? If this is the case, the answer to your procrastination may lie in making some major life changes. One man with ADD, employed as an attorney, re-ported that he spent huge portions of each workday procrastinating and accom-plishing very little. Upon reflection, he admitted to himself that he found the area of law in which he was engaged very boring. It was highly detailed, al-lowed little movement or interaction, and required tons of painstaking paper-work. A large part of his procrastination pattern was solved when he decided to take a cut in pay in order to practice in a field of law that was much more interesting to him.

Is your procrastination based on fear? Are you avoiding tasks because you're not very good at them or aren't sure how to accomplish them? Many students fall into such a trap. They avoid writing a paper or beginning a project because they aren't sure how to get started and feel overwhelmed. If this is the case, procrastination can often be overcome by enlisting the aid of someone who can help you get beyond the impasse that has you stuck. Help can come from a tutor, your professor, a friend with more knowledge in the area, or a co-worker.

Is your procrastination due to overbooking and fatigue? Many spouses of adults with ADD complain that their spouses never take care of things around the house or rarely take their share of responsibility for their children. This pattern may be worsened by overbooking and fatigue earlier in the day. If you have been stressed, overly busy, and late all day long, you will have little energy left to engage actively in your home life. You may need to examine a number of patterns in your life. Are you chronically deprived of sleep because you stay up too late at night? Are you overcommitted at the office? Is your fatigue worsened by lack of exercise or poor nutrition?

Chronic Lateness

Chronic lateness is such a strong pattern among adults with ADD that it is almost a hallmark of the disorder. This pattern is, of course, closely related to other time-management pitfalls. Lateness can occur due to:

1. *Scheduling your day too tightly*: There's not enough time to be on time.
   Solution: Plan to be early, or take work or reading to do once you're there.

2. *Overfocusing*: Some people find they are repeatedly late for appointments because they overfocused on an activity and lost track of the time.
   Solution: Set timers or ask for a reminder if you plan to engage in an activity on which you will become hyperfocused.

3. *Disorganization*: Another ADD pattern leading to late arrival is lack of advanced planning and organization; the process of getting ready to depart for an appointment, including gathering the items that will be needed for that meeting, isn't even begun until it is time to depart.
   Solution: just the same as for kids. Place the things you will need in your briefcase, or on the table next to the door, the night before. This should become part of your "daily planning session"—not just planning for your next day on paper—but preparing for it by gathering the items and documents you will need.

4. *Squeezing in "just one more thing"*: Many adults with ADD report that they are repeatedly late because they always try to do "one more thing" before leaving for their appointment, or they may even try to squeeze in an errand on the way.
   Solution: Write the "one more thing" down if you're afraid you'll forget it. Also become more aware of your impact on others. Many adults with ADD become so habituated to being late that they are insensitive to the effect it

has upon others and unaware of the negative attitude toward themselves generated by this behavior.

5. *Getting sidetracked*: Although it may sound contradictory, often when an adult with ADD has too much time before a scheduled event, he or she is even more likely to be late. For example, one woman reported that she tried to make all of her appointments first thing in the morning. If she scheduled a noon appointment, she was less likely to get ready in a timely, organized fashion because she had hours in which to prepare. As a result, she often found herself becoming involved in other activities and then still rushing at the last minute to shower and dress for her appointment.

   Solution: Keep your day more structured. It's hard to move from a "floating" mode to a focused mode. Get ready for your day first thing in the morning. ADD adults who work at home may be tempted to not shower, shave, or get dressed. Then if they have an appointment scheduled they rush to get ready at the last minute, and often arrive late. Set a timer to remind yourself to prepare for a scheduled event.

Distractibility

Distractibility is an ever-present threat, disrupting the best-laid plans for the day. Distractions may be external—interruptions, noise, phone calls—or they may just as likely be internal and self-generated. Many adults with ADD report that, once they have become distracted from a task, they find it is very difficult for them, requiring much time and energy, to effectively refocus on the task. For this reason it is critical that you learn to minimize distractions. External distracters are more clearly defined and often easier to eliminate. Turn off the phone, shut the door, use a sound screen machine, and so forth.

Internal distracters can be more difficult to manage because they sneak up on you unexpectedly. You can't tell yourself "Don't think about that!" Thoughts simply come to us, and a rapid flow of ideas is often typical of adults with ADD.

One technique for dealing with intrusive ideas is to keep your day planner with you at all times. If you are working on a project and find that you suddenly think of something that you need to do, write the thought down and continue with your current task until it is completed.

One man found it useful to program a timer to beep every twenty minutes. He used this auditory reminder as a cue to make sure he was "on task" and that he hadn't allowed himself, unwittingly, to wander off into some unrelated task.

Hyper-Focusing

Hyper-focusing may sound contradictory for someone with ADD. If a person has an "attention deficit" how can they focus intensely, for hours, on one activity? In actuality, ADD is not a "deficit" of attention, but a disorder in which individuals have much less control over their responses to stimuli. Individuals with ADD are often both overresponsive to random stimuli (distractible) and underresponsive to what should be salient stimuli (hyper-focused), depending on their stress level and the activity in which they are engaged.

One woman with ADD told a story of living in an old house during her graduate school years. She had become so hyper-focused on a paper that she was writing that she was completely unaware that the house had caught on fire and that hook-and-ladder trucks were on the scene to combat the blaze. She had missed the sirens and all the commotion and was finally discovered by firemen, working contentedly in her room while the kitchen at the back of the house was engulfed in flames!

Hyper-focusing can be a great gift if it is:

- used for positive, constructive activities.

- it is managed.

Hyper-focusing can be very detrimental if:

- it occurs primarily during escapist activities.

- it is not managed and therefore takes time away from other commitments.

- it results in ignoring important people in your life.

To manage your tendency to hyperfocus:

- Try to arrange your life and your career so that the things you love to do and on which you tend to hyper-focus are, in fact, things that will advance you in your career. In other words, choose something you love to do as your life's work.

- Set firm limits around activities on which you hyper-focus that are "escapist" activities (television, reading, gambling, "on-line" interacting, computer time).

- Establish alarms or other reminders to cue you when you need to break away from your hyper-focused activity.

PUT YOURSELF WHERE YOU'LL BE APPRECIATED

One of the most damaging effects of lifelong ADD is the relentless stream of negative feedback that many children with ADD experience from parents and teachers: "Haven't I told you a thousand times!" "What have you done now?" "Don't be so immature." "Settle down!" "You're just not trying hard enough." "Why do you leave everything to the last minute?" "Where were you! I told you to be here waiting for me." "Next time you lose your key it's coming out of your allowance!" Do any of these remarks sound familiar? Comments like these erode self-esteem and can easily lead a child to believe that he's destined to fail no matter how hard he tries. Young adults with ADD often continue to feel like failures because they have dropped out of school or haven't achieved as much as their siblings. Sadly, some adults with ADD internalize many of the negative messages they received as children. Such adults may remain in relationships where they are criticized or unappreciated, assuming that such is their lot in life.

The good news is that as an adult you have an opportunity to place yourself around people who appreciate you. You can choose to engage in activities that are a better match for your abilities. It's important to actively look for people who enjoy and appreciate your best traits. This doesn't mean that you don't want to change some of your ADD patterns. But living around people who are impatient, irritated, and frequently critical of your behavior is not likely to help you make positive changes.

If you are fortunate enough to have an adult ADD support group in your community, you may find the group to be a great resource as you come to terms with your ADD and learn to manage it. Having a support group may be one of the most important steps you can take to find a group of people whom you enjoy and who understand the struggles you experience.

CREATING A SUPPORTIVE LIVING ENVIRONMENT

One of the most critical factors determining how much you are affected by your ADD symptoms is the environment in which you operate. ADD symptoms tend to worsen in environments that have low structure and high stress. Conversely, ADD symptoms are minimized in environments that are less stressful and more structured. Listed below are some of the factors that you can control in order to minimize the negative impact of ADD on your daily functioning.

- **Sleep.** Try to get seven to eight hours of sleep each night.

- **Exercise.** Regular, vigorous exercise helps reduce tension and restlessness.

- **Diet.** Eat regularly; don't skip meals; hunger can intensify irritability, impatience and impulsivity; healthy eating habits are important as well.

- **Health.** Don't let yourself stay so busy and distracted that you ignore health problems; your ADD symptoms will tend to multiply under any stressful situation, including health problems.

- **Caffeine.** Keep caffeine to a minimum, especially if you are taking stimulant medication; caffeine can cause feelings of tension and jitteriness, irritability, and overreactions.

- **Stress.** The better you manage and minimize the stress in your life, the more your ADD symptoms will be under control.

- **Structure.** Try to build structured routines into your life. Because ADD tends to create disorder in your life, the more order you can build around you the better you will function.

- **Balance.** Many adults with ADD are prone to hyper-focus on one area of their life, to the exclusion of all other things. Routines are ignored, normal life-maintenance activities go undone, and chaos levels increase. Try to keep a balance between your personal and professional life; between your pleasurable escapes and necessary chores.

Sleep-Arousal Problems

Many people with ADD experience difficulty with sleep-arousal problems. They may be prone to feel sleepy during the day when they need to concentrate and focus. At night, many adults with ADD report that their mind is racing so fast that they are unable to fall asleep at a reasonable hour. Going to bed late sets the stage for exhaustion the following workday.

Some people deal with extreme "night-owl" tendencies by looking for work that allows a more flexible schedule. If you have a job that doesn't allow such flexibility, however, it is critical that you find ways to get adequate amounts of sleep. Being exhausted all week, getting only five hours of sleep or less, then trying to catch up on sleep over the weekend is a pattern of self-abuse that will increase ADD symptoms.

Getting to sleep at night:

1. Develop a regular bedtime. Our bodies fall asleep much more readily if they have been "programmed" to sleep at a certain hour.

2. Develop a relaxing bedtime routine.

3. Quit working or engaging in any stimulating activity one hour before bedtime.

4. Don't allow yourself to nap early in the evening.

5. Be careful not to take stimulant medication too late in the day.

6. Stay away from caffeine in the afternoon and evening.

7. Develop relaxation or meditation routines to help slow down your thoughts.

8. Consult your physician who is prescribing medication for ADD if all of these suggestions fail.

Stress Management

Stress exerts a strong negative influence on the functioning of adults with ADD. Times of high stress, including periods of increased demands, fatigue, illness, conflict, or frustration, tend to be periods in which the symptoms of ADD worsen. During periods of stress, the ADD adult is likely to be less organized, more absentminded, less efficient, and more prone to error and temper outbursts. In times of low stress, the functioning of ADD adults tends to improve. A good place to begin reducing the stress in your life is with a "stress assessment." Read the following list of potential stressors and rate yourself from 1 to 5 on each. Any area in which you rate yourself at 3 or higher is an area that needs to be stress-reduced, if possible.

Stress Assessment

Following is a list of areas of potential stress in your life. As you read through this list, there may be other stressors in your life that come to mind. Please add any additional stressors to this list as you think of them. Then rate your stress level on each item.

1. Not a stressor in my life

2. A mild source of stress

3. A moderate source of stress

4. A significant source of stress

5. A crisis area in my life causing tremendous stress

Finances

_____ In debt
_____ Make too many impulse purchases
_____ Keep poor financial records
_____ Don't budget my money
_____ Little or no savings for emergencies
_____ Problems filing tax returns/paying taxes owed
_____ Other

Family

_____ Marital problems
_____ Child behavior problems
_____ Poor parenting skills
_____ Family crisis: illness, death, divorce
_____ Responsibility for aging parent
_____ Other

Career

_____ Stress at work
_____ Unemployed
_____ Interpersonal conflicts at work
_____ Poor job match
_____ Long commute
_____ Long work hours
_____ Other

Health

_____ Major illness
_____ Chronic health problem

_____ Chronic health problem of family member
_____ Poor health habits
_____ Chronic sleep difficulties
_____ Other

General Stressors

_____ Chronic overcommitment
_____ Poor time management
_____ Poor organization
_____ Always behind on daily chores—laundry, meals, cleaning
_____ Too many changes
_____ Domino effect—unsolved problems causing more problems
_____ Other

Internal Stressors

_____ High anxiety
_____ Depression
_____ Fear of failure
_____ Feelings of inadequacy
_____ Unable to relax
_____ Other

After identifying the stressors in your life, take each one and think about ways to reduce or eliminate that stressor. You may feel locked into a lifestyle and believe that you have few options. Chances are, after some creative problem solving, you will think of lots of solutions. Some may be immediate solutions; others may take longer to bring about.

Some ways to reduce stressors include:

- **Look for ways to simplify your life.** These might include changing jobs, moving closer to work, moving to a townhouse or apartment, and eliminating some commitments.

- **Think of things you can delegate to others.** This might include hiring someone who can perform tasks that are particularly stressful for you.

- **Avoid situations that are stressful for you.** Change your work hours to avoid rush hour. Try to shop during off-peak hours. Plan less elaborate holiday celebrations. Take friends out for dinner rather than entertaining at home. Don't take the kids with you to the grocery. Create a "quiet zone" in your home.

- **Learn stress reduction techniques.** Train yourself in relaxation exercises. They are simple, effective, and can be learned easily. The more you practice them the more effective they become. They include muscle relaxation techniques, imagery techniques, and deep breathing exercises. Soothing music can also enhance relaxation.

Money Management

Poor money management is quite often a problem for adults with ADD. Often these problems result from impulse purchases, overspending, lack of long-term planning, and poor record keeping. Unfortunately, most financial management programs suggest highly detailed record keeping and micro-management of expenditures, neither of which are very compatible with ADD tendencies.

Good money management for ADD adults needs to rely on a few, simple principles.

- **Keep it simple.** Have as few bills as possible. Don't keep accounts at every store in town. Use only one charge card. That way it's much easier to keep track of charges.

- **Make it automatic.** Have your paycheck automatically deposited. Have as many bills as possible automatically paid by your bank. Arrange for an automatic savings deposit at the first of each month.

- **Minimize impulsive overspending.** Take out cash only once a week, then budget that cash for the week. Don't shop for recreation. Shop by phone for the best price. Have it delivered by mail to eliminate impulsive purchasing.

Coping with Hyperactivity

To minimize the negative effects on yourself from hyperactivity:

- Take frequent breaks that allow movement

- Get regular daily exercise

- Carefully monitor the stress level of your day

- Monitor your caffeine intake

To minimize the impact of your hyperactivity on others:

- Don't pressure others to keep up with you

- Go out for a run if you're feeling wound up

- Monitor yourself when you're interacting with others

- Take a deep breath and slow down if you're talking too fast

- Try not to let yourself become overstimulated

COPING WITH IMPULSIVITY

Highly Stimulating Situations

Watch yourself and become better aware of the situations in which you are likely to become impulsive. Impulsive interrupting, for example, may be more likely to happen in highly stimulating social environments. You may be able to control this better when you interact one-on-one.

Times of Emotional Intensity

Other impulsive behaviors result from emotional intensity. Losing your temper, crying, cursing, or making an impulsive remark you may later regret are more likely to happen when impulse control is down due to alcohol, when hormones are dysregulated due to the menstrual cycle, or when impulse control is reduced due to fatigue or stress. Try to avoid situations in which you lose emotional control.

Surrounding Yourself with Temptation

Still other impulsive behaviors occur because we place ourselves in temptation's way. Impulsive eating is most likely to occur when we have immediate access to tempting food. Impulsive spending occurs when we "window shop" in our favorite stores.

MEMORY TECHNIQUES

Memory difficulties are very common for adults with ADD. Typically these memory difficulties are related to distractibility. In order for information to be remembered, you must first pay attention to it.

Write What You Hear, Say What You Read

In situations calling for prolonged attention, such as listening to a lecture or reading a book, attention tends to be intermittent at best, causing some adults with ADD to experience tremendous difficulty in recalling things that they have heard or read. There are a number of things you can do to enhance your memory in these types of circumstances. People tend to recall information better if they have received it in more than one sensory modality—for example, seeing and hearing information simultaneously.

Reading aloud can enhance attention and can assist retention in long-term memory as well. Similarly, it can help focus attention and aid memory if you take notes while listening. These are the types of memory abilities most often called for in academic settings. There are other memory techniques that can be learned to assist with academic study. If you are in a learning situation, or plan to return to school, practicing these techniques may help. Working with a tutor to acquire other memory techniques may also be useful.

A Short Note Is Better Than a Long Memory!

Memory problems also can greatly interfere with daily living. Many adults with ADD have difficulty registering and retaining things they have been told. This can cause tremendous frustrations, for the adult with ADD as well as for the co-worker, friend, or family member whose words were forgotten. The most effective tool to aid poor auditory memory is to always write things down, no matter how sure you are that you'll remember them. If you have developed the habit of keeping your day planner with you at all times, then the obvious and best place to write things down is in your day planner.

Message Centers

Tell your family, friends, and co-workers to give you information in writing. Send information at work by E-mail and FAX. At home, ask everyone to write you a note. Every ADD home should have a message center. The kitchen, next to the phone, is the best place—somewhere central where everyone is in the habit of checking regularly.

Develop Routines

Rituals and routines are "overlearned" behaviors that place very little demand on attention and memory. We go through routines automatically. Many parts of your day, such as preparation for work or school in the morning and preparation for bed at night, should be routinized. Other routines that are important are a daily planning period at the beginning of the day and a second planning period just before returning home at night. This second planning period is a time to shift from thinking of work responsibilities to thinking about personal commitments.

Visual Prompts

Many people with ADD find that visual reminders are very helpful. If you need to mail a letter in the morning, place it in a prominent place near the door you will exit. Place reminder notes in places you will notice. Put things you need to take to work in the morning right next to the front door. It can be very helpful to keep a pad of "sticky notes" in your day planner. That will allow you to always write yourself a note and place it in a prominent place.

Electronic Reminders

A watch with multiple programmable "beeps" can be useful to remind yourself to do things that must occur at certain intervals (such as taking medication) or to remind yourself to leave for a scheduled event. There are computer programs designed as organizers that also offer auditory reminders of events that need to be recalled.

Auditory Prompts

Some people find it useful to leave themselves messages. Some have learned to routinely leave messages for themselves at work on their voice mail and to leave reminders for themselves at home on their own answering machine. Several devices have been developed recently that serve as tiny, hand-held recorders designed for recording reminders to yourself that you can replay later.

PROBLEM-SOLVING APPROACHES

Many adults with ADD have a tendency to respond to problems in an unplanned and impulsive fashion. This can lead to a long series of misguided decisions. Other ADD adults have tremendous difficulty reaching any decision at all. Their imaginations are carried away by potential solutions and potential pitfalls. They become so confused by the array of possibilities that they end by making no decision at all or by waiting until a decision is made by someone else. Neither of these approaches is very effective.

The next time you have a decision to make, it may be helpful to go through the problem-solving steps outlined here. For those who are impulsive, this approach will force you to slow down long enough to think of possible alternatives. For those who become paralyzed by possibilities, following these steps will help move you from the idea stage to the action stage.

1. Define the problem. A careful analysis of the problem, along with the opportunity to talk over the problem with someone else, may help you to see the problem in a new way.

2. Write a list of possible solutions. Brainstorm with someone if you can. Don't eliminate any possibilities at this point. Be creative. Be silly. Don't shoot holes in any of your ideas at this stage. (Many adults with ADD have a very rapid flow of ideas and are great at this type of brainstorming.)

3. Consider each of your solutions. Rank them in order. Don't get obsessive at this stage about which solution is the very best.

4. Choose one of the solutions you think is best and try it.

5. Analyze the results of your trial. Was it a success? If not, why not?

6. Try an alternate solution if the results of the first trial weren't to your liking.

7. Continue in this fashion—testing, analyzing, correcting for errors, and adding new information if it becomes available. Try again.

YOUR OPTIMAL "WINDOW" OF STIMULATION

Many adults with ADD find that they have a "window" of optimal stimulation. That is, they function best within a certain range of stimulation. When they are understimulated, they may feel lethargic, moody, and unmotivated. Some ADDers who feel bored and understimulated may, without realizing what has prompted them, start a quarrel with a family member just to increase their stimulation level. It is important to think of positive ways to stimulate yourself. Otherwise you could find yourself stirring up trouble!

When overstimulated, some ADD adults find themselves behaving impulsively, feeling irritable, overreacting to annoyances, and making more mistakes than usual. When stimulation is just right, they find that they are at their best, feeling motivated, interested, and energetic.

It is very important that you think about your "optimal window" when making major life choices. If your optimal level is high, you may need an urban environment and a fairly challenging work environment. If you are easily overstressed, you may need to work fewer hours and live in a small-town environment with a short commute. Your home environment is important, too. If you need to retreat to a "quiet zone" at home to maintain your equilibrium, think carefully about the size and design of your living space.

Your "optimal zone" will fluctuate during the day depending upon daily stresses. Try to monitor yourself. Find a way to temporarily "retreat" when overstimulated. Look for positive ways to engage yourself when feeling understimulated.

Getting Organized

Disorganization is often one of the major struggles for adults with ADD, which makes sense if you review a list of traits of adults with ADD and then compare those traits to the behaviors required for good organization:

ADD	*Organized*
Impulsive	Planner
Reactive	Proactive
Distractible	Focused
Plays it "by ear"	Develops a plan
Jumps from one thing to the next	Carries task through to completion

Does this mean that if you have ADD you can never be organized? No, not at all, but it does mean that organization will require greater effort on your part. In fact, some adults with ADD have so overfocused on organization in their attempts to manage their ADD that they become somewhat obsessional and perfectionistic.

Combatting the "Enemies" of Organization

1. **Lack of task completion.** If you change only one thing in your attempts to become better organized, you should learn to recognize and work toward task completion. This is true for all things, large and small, for example: Hang up your coat, or purse, don't put it somewhere "for now." "For now" usually becomes "forever" in ADD households. Put the stamp on the letter and mail it. Don't say, "I'll just leave this little bit to finish later." Much of the clutter and disorganization in the lives of adults with ADD is the result of hundreds of uncompleted tasks, both great and small.

2. **Poor memory.** Memory problems, combined with quitting tasks in midstream, create chaos. Because you are not likely to remember to get back to all of the things you said you'd get back to, you're much better off completing them now.

3. **I'd better save this. I might need it.** Decision making is often very hard

for adults with ADD. It feels less risky to hang on to things than to get rid of them. As a result of this kind of thinking, the offices and households of many adults with ADD have become hopelessly and chaotically cluttered with books, magazines, papers, and paraphernalia relating to long-abandoned hobbies. Give yourself a cutoff date. If you haven't read it, worn it, or used it in two years, pitch it. Sometimes it can be very helpful to enlist the aid of a friend or relative who is less attached to your clutter to assist with the process of unburdening yourself.

4. **Relying on visual cues.** Again, due to poor memory, many adults with ADD leave things on tables, dressers, even floors, as a reminder of where to find the item, or as a reminder that some task needs to be accomplished. Visual cues are very helpful aids for adults with ADD; however, they don't need to be disorderly.

    For example, the desks of many ADDers are cluttered with folders and papers relating to tasks that are in progress or that need to be done. Many adults feel that if they file the material, they will either forget where they filed it or that they need to take care of it. One good solution that still provides visual cues is the use of a "file cart": This is a trolley, on wheels, which contains a small group of active files. Because the trolley is open, the tabs of the files are in plain, accessible view. Hanging files of different colors can be used as a quick guide to different types of files or projects. A quick visual scan of the file tabs will lead you to the desired paper or folder much more readily than if you had to dig through a stack of papers and folders piled on your desk.

    Other visual displays can work well too, without being disordered. Some adults with ADD, for example, find their clothing much more accessible if they organize their clothes into plastic crates that are neatly stacked in their closet rather than putting clothing away in closed drawers.

5. **I'll do it in a minute.** Who are you kidding? Many adults with ADD report that they can become sidetracked from a task during the time it takes to walk downstairs in their house. If you can't stay focused for thirty seconds, how will you remember to "do it later"? Adults with ADD need to live by the creed *"Do it now or write it down (in your day planner)."*

6. **"The world is so full of a number of things, I'm sure we should all be as happy as kings."** (From an English nursery rhyme.) For many adults with ADD, their world becomes so full of interesting things that desks,

households, and lives can become dysfunctional. A common gift among those with ADD is a spontaneous flood of ideas, many of which are worthwhile and creative. To maintain any order in your life, however, there needs to be some mechanism in place to manage the flow of these ideas. New ideas typically shove aside old ideas, leading to a life strewn with incomplete projects.

One way to manage this idea flood is to maintain a place in your day planner in which you list new projects or ideas. As you complete a task you can refer to this list to choose a new one. More likely than not, you will find that in the meantime you've had yet another new idea and that even the ideas on your list feel "old" and less appealing!

SO WHERE DO I BEGIN?

The most important place to begin is to realize that you are learning to live your life in a very different fashion and that this learning process will take time and practice. It is very useful to work on organizational skills over a period of months with the aid of a counselor, therapist, or coach to help keep you on track.

Don't feel you have to do it all on your own. Pick an area of your life to begin, and then work with someone about how to organize that particular area or project.

One of the most critical tools of life management will be your day planner. In fact, your day planner is the best place to schedule all of the activities required to better organize your time and your living space.

And remember, your goal is not to "get" organized but to "be" organized, so start small, build habits, and let the habits of organization gradually spread to other areas of your life.

5

Building a Strong Marriage

Building a Strong Marriage

ADD can have a profound, and often troubling, impact on a marriage if it is not recognized, understood, and accepted by both partners. Acceptance can be the most important, and sometimes the most difficult, step to reach. With acceptance, both partners can work together to find solutions to ADD issues that affect their marriage.

EXPLAINING ADD TO YOUR SPOUSE

Sometimes an adult comes to suspect that he or she may have ADD after the problems caused by ADD have already eroded a sense of trust and mutual cooperation in his/her marriage. If unrecognized ADD has led to patterns of chronic lateness, forgetfulness, preoccupation, and apparent insensitivity, a spouse may react with understandable skepticism when his or her partner suddenly announces that she or he may have ADD. This can be especially true if the idea of ADD is presented as, "See, it's not my fault; I've had ADD all these years and didn't know it." ADD needs to be presented in a constructive light. Diagnosing the ADD is only the first step toward finding solutions.

If you suspect that you may have ADD, try to include your spouse in the process of becoming educated about ADD. Share books, magazine articles, and any other information you may have. Encourage your spouse to attend support group meetings with you. If you are working with a therapist, it may be very helpful to include your spouse in some of the sessions, particularly sessions focused on seeking solutions to problems that affect your partner.

Engage your spouse as your ally in your efforts to meet the challenge of ADD. He or she can be an enormous asset as you attempt to monitor the effects of medication and as you try to understand and change certain patterns of behavior. Individuals with ADD are often inaccurate self-observers. By bringing your spouse into the process, you can benefit from his or her observations. This does not mean that the ADD is not "your" issue. There certainly will be many issues that do not directly involve your spouse. But where your spouse is directly affected by your ADD, he or she needs to be brought into the process of recognizing problems and finding solutions.

If your partner appears skeptical or uninterested in ADD at first, don't despair. Chances are that you have jumped on bandwagons before. Your spouse may assume that ADD is just your latest fad. If you persist in taking your ADD seriously, and if you continue to share what you learn with your spouse, chances are good that he or she will join you to work against the negative effects of ADD on your marriage.

WHEN YOUR SPOUSE SEES ADD AS AN "EXCUSE"

It may be tempting to use ADD as an excuse, a proof that it's not your fault when you are late, lose track of time, forget to call home, or leave things to the last minute. Understandably, many spouses may become resentful of the ADD label. Spouses of adults with ADD may fear that the ADD label leaves them holding the bag of responsibilities forever, while their partner has a note from the doctor saying "He or she can't help it. Don't blame him/her!"

For your partner to accept your ADD diagnosis, it needs to be accompanied by a blueprint for change. This blueprint should include a list of problematic behavior patterns, along with a list of strategies and coping mechanisms for dealing with those problems. You need to show your spouse that you plan to use your ADD diagnosis to *solve* problems rather than to absolve yourself of responsibility for problems. When you work to meet the challenges of ADD, it is more likely that your spouse will be receptive to the ADD diagnosis.

Responding to the Needs of the Non-ADD Spouse

The non-ADD spouse's needs may be somewhat ignored as his or her partner's ADD is diagnosed and treated. For the treatment to be successful, the non-ADD partner must be heard, understood, and supported as well. Often the non-ADD partner has long since reached a point of burnout in the marriage as he or she has valiantly struggled to keep the marriage and family afloat. If the initial stages of treatment focus only on the needs of the spouse with ADD, the non-ADD spouse may withdraw in anger: "I've carried the whole load all these years, and now I'm supposed to continue to be supportive and understanding! Well, what about me? Who's going to think about what I need?"

One such spouse, whose husband sought an ADD diagnosis, came to only a single session. Her husband had played a very passive, dependent role in their marriage for years. She had been opposed to his seeking an ADD evaluation, fearing that it would only give him a medical excuse for his irresponsible behavior. Her resentment was so strong that when she heard the ADD diagnosis she left the session, sure that her worst fears had come true. Sadly, she was unable to benefit from the treatment following her husband's initial diagnosis.

Another ADD spouse was so angry at her husband that she refused to become involved in any aspect of diagnosis or treatment. She had entered therapy herself prior to her husband's ADD diagnosis and had slowly learned to set boundaries and limits with her husband. Only after several months, when her husband showed a positive response to medication and had made a genuine effort to change problematic behaviors, did she agree to join him in ADD-focused couples counseling.

Spouses of ADD adults have their own set of emotional reactions, including denial, anger, grief, and acceptance, as they learn that their spouse has a medical condition that can be treated, but not cured, and that will present challenges, to some extent, for the rest of their married life. Many spouses go through periods of real sadness and despair before they are emotionally ready to begin the process of realistic acceptance and problem solving. Spouses need to stick around long enough to hear the good news. They have been living with an ADD spouse for years without knowing it. The ADD diagnosis is the first step in treating the ADD and in reducing, if not eliminating, many of the problems.

WHEN YOU SUSPECT YOUR SPOUSE HAS ADD

If you suspect that your partner may have ADD, it is important that you introduce the subject in a nonjudgmental way. If ADD-like issues have already led to marital conflict, it can be very difficult to bring up ADD in a manner that feels supportive or constructive. Sometimes a discussion of ADD may happen spontaneously in response to a television program both partners view together. If you feel strongly that ADD may play a major role in your marital problems, sessions with a marital counselor may improve communication and allow a constructive discussion of ADD.

Be careful to avoid the "blame game" when you introduce the topic of ADD. If your spouse feels that you are pointing the finger at his or her ADD as the cause of all the problems in the marriage, he or she will be much less open to the idea of ADD. It is essential that ADD issues be talked about in a constructive rather than destructive fashion.

WHEN SEEKING A MARRIAGE PARTNER

Adults with ADD come in all shapes, sizes, and personalities. ADD does not affect everyone in the same way. Nevertheless, if you are not married and you have ADD, it is important to take your ADD into account when you consider marriage. There are some important factors to consider about yourself.

Adults with ADD can be full of interesting contradictions! They often fluctuate between a need for variety and stimulation and a need for order and control. As a result, adults with ADD are sometimes attracted to persons like themselves who are active, lively, unpredictable, and imaginative. Other ADD adults, due to internal and external disorganization, are attracted to individuals who are more calm, orderly, and organized.

Marriages between individuals who both share traits of ADD can be very stimulating and exciting but are also likely to be disorganized and full of the problems caused by two people who leave lots of things until the last minute. For such a marriage to work, both partners need to have a fairly high tolerance for stress, a high degree of flexibility, and a flair for crisis management. A marriage between two adults with ADD may be volatile if both partners tend toward stubbornness and emotional intensity but can also provide mutual understanding and support because both partners can understand the other's ADD traits. Adding children to such a marriage means a high likelihood of children with ADD and almost certainly a lifestyle of creative chaos!

A very different choice made by some adults with ADD is a relationship that borders on codependency. These ADDers are drawn to people who will take care of all the details of life for them. In reasonable measure, it's not a bad idea to marry someone who can complement your strengths and weaknesses. If the imbalance becomes too exaggerated, though, the marriage may begin to feel like a parent–child relationship in which the ADD adult feels nagged and controlled and the partner feels overburdened with responsibility. This relationship may deteriorate into one of criticism and resentment on both sides.

Key Issues When Considering Marriage

1. **Hypersensitivity.** Many adults with ADD are extra-sensitive to criticism because they have experienced a barrage of negative remarks throughout their growing up years. If this is true for you, it may be especially important to choose a spouse who is calm and tolerant.

2. **Emotional volatility.** Many, but not all, adults with ADD are prone to react with intense emotions to upsets and frustrations. Some of this can be reduced through medication and through psychotherapy. If this is a pattern in your life, though, you should think carefully about looking for a partner who will not intensify this problem with his or her own emotional volatility.

3. **Need for order.** Some adults compensate for their ADD by developing an orderly and routinized life. Very specific habits and patterns may be a good and even necessary way to compensate for disorganization and forgetfulness. Some ADD adults may even appear to be rigid and inflexible because of their tendency to adhere to their rituals. If order and predictability are strong needs, you may be a poor match for someone who is more spontaneous and disorganized by nature.

4. **Low stress tolerance.** Too many adults with ADD don't plan ahead and find themselves enmeshed in a lifestyle that includes several children, a high-stress job, big-city traffic, a long commute, and a high mortgage pay-

ment. Many ADD adults react to such stress by withdrawal, which can create serious problems within a marriage. If you are an adult who becomes easily stressed and anxious, take care to build a low-stress lifestyle for yourself and choose a partner who is looking for the same.

5. **Need for excitement and stimulation.** Some adults with ADD feel a strong drive for stimulation and activity. If you are prone to impulsive decisions, if you become quickly bored and want to change jobs or homes with frequency, take care to choose a partner who enjoys being swept along by your excitement. If your partner needs more stability and permanence, a tug-of-war is likely to develop. Your marriage may begin to feel like an anchor that you struggle to drag along in your wake.

6. **Seeking low stress and high stimulation.** Just to complicate things, there are adults with ADD who have low stress tolerance but at the same time are easily bored. For these people, life management and choice of a compatible mate are especially challenging. Such individuals may feel highly anxious if bills are unpaid, if the car breaks down unexpectedly, or if there are interpersonal conflicts in their life. On the other hand, they feel bored and restless if "nothing is happening." Tolerant, adaptable mates and a clear understanding of the differences between "good" and "bad" stimulation are important in order to prevent life from becoming a roller-coaster ride.

The more you learn about yourself through psychotherapy and educating yourself about adult ADD, the better your chances are of making a good choice of marriage partner.

OVERDEPENDENCE ON YOUR NON-ADD PARTNER

One of the most common causes of stress in ADD marriages comes from a pattern of increasing overreliance on the non-ADD partner. Such a pattern can develop only with the active participation of both partners, and the solution needs to be worked on by both partners as well.

A pattern of co-dependency may develop between an ADD adult and his or her spouse: The non-ADD adult has the gratification of feeling important, needed, competent, and in control while the ADD spouse may fall into a pattern of habitual overdependency. Over time, however, these patterns may become too exaggerated and ingrained. The non-ADD spouse may begin to act and feel more like a parent than a spouse. The ADD partner resents the parentlike orders and criticisms, and the marriage becomes increasingly dysfunctional.

Building a Complementary Partnership

To avoid such dysfunctional patterns in your marriage, work toward complementarity in your marriage. There is an important difference between a complementary and a co-dependent marriage. In a co-dependent marriage, one partner habitually underfunctions while the other habitually overfunctions. In a complementary marriage, both partners are aware of their differences and of their own strengths and weaknesses. They work toward developing complementary roles and responsibilities. Many co-dependent ADD marriages can benefit from marital counseling to help each partner recognize his or her contributions to their co-dependent patterns and to help them develop healthier, more balanced ways of working together.

PATTERNS OF BLAME AND SHAME

Patterns of blame and anger that develop in ADD marriages can be very destructive over time. Unfortunately, some couples do not seek help until these patterns are so powerful that they are difficult to alter. In one such ADD marriage, the husband and wife ran a small business together. The husband's ADD led him to be rather impulsive, restless, and poor at keeping accurate records. His wife, who was more cautious and detail oriented, would have been much better suited to keep the business accounts and records. The husband had developed a pattern of making secretive business decisions, anticipating that his wife would veto them if he discussed them with her. When the results of some of these decisions were disastrous, he responded by making ever more desperate attempts to hide financial problems from his wife. Unfortunately, the couple did not seek treatment for ADD or for marital problems related to ADD until they were near bankruptcy. The husband's sense of shame and the wife's mistrust and lack of respect for her husband were so strong that they were unable to honestly talk about their problems and work toward constructive solutions.

In most ADD marriages these patterns are not so extreme. A marriage counselor needs to work with ADD couples to help the non-ADD spouse understand that many of the ADD patterns are not under full voluntary control and at the same time help the ADD spouse to take more responsibility for developing coping strategies.

PROBLEMS WITH EMOTIONAL INTIMACY

Do any of the following sound familiar?

"You are never around when I need you."

"Whenever I'm talking to you, it feels like your mind is somewhere else."

"A few minutes after I start a conversation you turn on the TV or leave the room."

"Whenever we have a problem, you disappear or say you don't want to talk about it."

If these phrases ring true, problems with emotional intimacy in your marriage may be largely the result of ADD. By considering some typical ADD traits, it is easy to understand why. Hyperactivity, restlessness, distractibility, and preoccupation can all work against emotional intimacy. In addition, many adults with ADD are poor at reading nonverbal cues. The ADD spouse may feel, "How could she not know that I'm upset over problems at work?" or "How could he not realize that I'm sad?" Additionally, many ADDers are less aware of their own tone of voice and body language and may give a false impression that they are angry or irritated.

Building Emotional Intimacy

1. **Make "together time" a daily habit.** Set a particular time of day, one that is less likely to be canceled by competing activities, and stick to it. Even a regular 15-minute period each day that is given top priority by both partners is a step in the right direction. Don't rely on the chance that such times will develop spontaneously. If they do, then so much the better. But make sure your marriage is nourished by scheduling time together.

2. **Make your "together time" positive.** In some ADD families there are so many minor crises and problems that communication time can become "problem time." Many adults with ADD report that they avoid time with their spouse because almost all of their interaction is negative, focusing on what the ADD partner has neglected to do once again. Problem solving will go more smoothly after you build a positive base for your marriage through spending time together.

3. **Be active together.** If the ADD partner is restless or hyperactive, he or she may not feel comfortable "just talking." Sit in a hot tub, swing in the hammock, take a stroll around the block, and you may find that talk flows much more easily.

4. **Try to keep blame and anger separate from problem solving.** Spouses of ADDers can't always be tolerant and understanding! There are times when you need to express anger and frustration. Make it brief and to the point, though. Your ADD spouse isn't likely to stick around for a half-hour diatribe, and even if she would, it's not likely to be constructive. Express your anger when you need to, but wait for calmer times to look for solutions.

5. **Look for interests and activities to share.** Some ADD partners are too restless to just "hang out" but would like to spend time together with their spouse engaged in some sport or activity.

PROBLEMS WITH SEXUAL INTIMACY

Many of the issues that can interfere with emotional intimacy affect sexual intimacy as well. If your partner feels tense, restless, irritable, preoccupied, or distracted, chances are that sexual contact will not occur or will be unsatisfying if it does occur. If sexual contact with your partner is infrequent or unsatisfying, you might find some of the following techniques to be helpful.

1. **Relaxation time.** All couples need relaxation time, but many adults with ADD become so tense and preoccupied that they have difficulty unwinding. Bathing or showering together, meditating together, or massaging each other can help create an atmosphere more conducive to physical intimacy.

2. **Getaways.** An overnight or weekend getaway is good for all couples who

find themselves caught up in the daily whirlwind of activities, but it may be even more crucial for ADD couples. Distractibility and preoccupation are such constant companions for adults with ADD that a brief and frequent getaway may be just what your marriage needs in order for you and your spouse to reconnect with each other. ADD adults who are prone to rush through sexual relations, leaving their partner feeling unsatisfied, may be able to slow down and enjoy a more prolonged sensual experience away from the pressure and distractions of daily living.

3. **Boredom and need for variety.** For some people with ADD, restlessness and rapid boredom are facts of life, which can take a difficult toll on long-term relationships. No matter how attractive or interesting a marriage partner may be, an ADD adult may find himself feeling dissatisfied. Couples can recognize and respond to it this situation by degrees through introducing variety into their sex life, experimenting with changes in location, position, and circumstance. Spontaneity and surprise may increase excitement as well. Both partners need to feel comfortable with the degree of experimentation and change. It is crucial that the non-ADD spouse realize that this need for added stimulation is not a reflection on him or her, but is a built-in aspect of the partner's ADD.

4. **Honest communication.** It is difficult for many couples to comfortably communicate their sexual needs and desires to each other, but it's essential for developing satisfying sexual interactions. An ADD partner, in particular, may need more direct communication because he or she may not pick up as readily on more subtle cues. Lynn Weiss, in her book *Attention Deficit Disorder in Adults: Practical Help for Sufferers and Their Spouses,* observes that many ADD adults are hypersensitive to various tactile stimulations. Rhythmic stroking, which might be considered soothing or sexual by some people, may feel annoying or irritating to some ADD adults. Such reactions need to be expressed matter-of-factly so that they don't become misinterpreted as "you don't want me to touch you" by the non-ADD spouse.

5. **Learn to recognize ADD patterns and not to misinterpret them.** One woman married to a husband with ADD complained about their infrequent sex life. Her husband often worked at his computer in the evenings, sometimes not coming to bed until long after she was asleep. She felt hurt and rejected despite her husband's assurance that he loved and cared for her. Through ADD-focused counseling, she came to recognize her husband's powerful tendency to become "hyper-focused" on his computer work. They

now have an agreement that she will remind him at 9 P.M. that it is "couple time." They both appreciate this sharing time at the end of the evening, and the period of mutual relaxation has led to more frequent and more satisfying sex between them.

PROBLEMS WITH COMMUNICATION

Communication difficulties are common between ADD adults and the people with whom they work and live. Patterns such as interrupting, monologuing, making non-sequitur remarks, and tuning out may be merely difficult or annoying for co-workers or friends. These same patterns can prove devastating in a more intimate relationship.

Do any of the following sound familiar?

"You never listen to me".
"You never told me you were going to…"
"I already told you that."
"If you really listened to me you would realize…"
"Don't interrupt me!"
"Talk *to* me, not *at* me!"

Although there are no magic solutions, here are some techniques which may improve communication in your relationship.

Communication Tips for ADD Adults

1. **If you are a chronic interrupter, learn to catch yourself.** Don't expect perfection of yourself. Sometimes, especially when you're wound up about a topic, you'll be prone to interrupt. But catching yourself and apologizing will tell your partner that you value what he or she is saying.

2. **If you interrupt because of fear that you'll forget, develop the habit of writing a brief note.** Tell your partner that you are writing the note so that you won't have to interrupt, then give your full attention to what he or she is saying.

3. **If you find your mind wandering, practice "active listening."** An ac-

tive listener looks at the person who is talking, nods, or gives other nonverbal reactions to indicate interest and response and asks questions or repeats back to the speaker what he has heard to check for accuracy.

4. **Tell your partner when you are too tired to really listen.** Let him know that now is not a good time but that you'd like to hear what he has to say when you are more rested.

5. **Catch yourself when you start on a long monologue.** Some ADDers love to talk and are not very sensitive to the interest level of those who are listening. Look for signs of restlessness or disinterest in your listener. Apologize if you catch yourself "talking someone's ear off."

6. **Take stock of your overall lifestyle.** If you are usually too tired to talk, then you need to think about reducing stress in other parts of your life. Your marriage needs and deserves energy and attention. ADDers who spend all of their energy at work do so at great emotional cost to their families.

Communication Tips for the Non-ADD Partner

1. **Realize the problem is ADD, not me.** It can't be stated too often how important it is for the non-ADD partner to understand that these patterns are not entirely under voluntary control and, most important, are not a reflection of lack of caring on the spouse's part.

2. **Be sensitive to your spouse's fatigue or stress level.** Often the end of the day, just after work, is a difficult time for ADD adults to communicate well. Fatigue and stress, both of which interfere with ability to concentrate, are at their peak. Look for the best times to communicate with your spouse and set those aside for "together time."

3. **If you like to share the events of the day in great detail, you may need to share them with someone else.** Some ADD adults feel trapped by long accounts of events that don't interest them.

4. **Develop common concerns and interests and talk about those.** ADD adults have much more difficulty than others politely listening to things that don't interest them. The best way to have long enjoyable conversations with an ADD adult is to talk together about things that interest you both. When you share clubs, hobbies, projects, sports activities or activities with the kids, you'll have much more to talk about.

5. **Try to keep communication about problems short, constructive, and solution focused.** Expressions of anger and frustration about recurrent problems in your marriage are healthy and inevitable. Don't try to prolong them, though, and don't expect good problem solving to immediately follow emotional upsets. Remember, ADDers often react very strongly to emotional situations and may need time to retreat and cool off before more constructive communication can take place.

Sharing Responsibilities

Juggling multiple roles is often difficult for adults with ADD. Housewives with ADD have one of the most difficult jobs in the world as a result. For those who work outside the home, distractibility, stress, fatigue, and absentmindedness often leave them with little energy for responsibilities on the home front. Sometimes chores at home go undone because of poor time management at work. At other times, they are left undone due to procrastination. Many ADD adults report that they have a strong tendency to dive into escapist activities at home such as television, movie videos, computer on-line services, computer games, books, magazines, catalogs, and the like. When the ADD adult is single, these patterns lead to disorganization and chaos at home. When the ADD adult is married, these patterns can result in chronic anger and resentment in the spouse who is "left holding the bag."

Do any of the following sound familiar?

"I can't count on you!"
"I'm not your mother/father!"
"You're always late!"
"Why do I have to ask you a hundred times?"
"Remember, they're *our* children, not *my* children."
"What have you been doing all day, anyway?"
"Why is it always up to me?"

It can be tempting and easy to fall into relying on a non-ADD partner to take care of things. The non-ADD spouse needs to realize, though, that this is not a clever plot on the part of the ADD spouse, but a reflection of great difficulty with organization, time management, and motivation. If you weren't there to take care of things, many of these things would simply never get done by your ADD spouse. In fact, there are many single ADD adults whose households and finances are in chaos and whose taxes are never filed on time. So, if you're married to a lovable but utterly disorganized person, what's to be done? Here are some ideas.

For the ADD Spouse

1. **Are you a "couch potato" at the end of the day?** You may need to look at overcommitments at work in order to have more energy to participate in home life.

2. **Do you leave the home front to your spouse?** Many non-ADD spouses feel that their partners leave most of the planning and decision making up to them at home because all of their energy and creativity is devoted to work. Save some of that "ADD creativity" and initiative for your marriage. One spouse of an ADDer reported, with happy amazement, that after her husband entered treatment for his ADD, he actually began to notice things around the house and began to take care of things on his own initiative. It was only then that the ADD husband began to realize how heavy a burden his wife had carried for years while he had been preoccupied with work.

3. **Do you gravitate toward "great escapes" at home?** Many adults with ADD lose themselves in interests or hobbies for hours, unable to drag themselves away to take care of daily tasks. These activities can take on an almost addictive quality. Some of these addictive pursuits include television, reading, computers, crafts, and hobbies. If you are a "great escaper," you'll need to take charge of these patterns and not allow yourself to escape into them until you have taken care of your life-management tasks for the day. Take on this responsibility yourself. Don't wait until your spouse is forced into nagging you. That's an old destructive pattern that ends with both of you feeling angry.

For the Non-ADD Spouse

1. **Own your own priorities.** You need to establish a compromise between your standards and your spouse's. If a high degree of order is important to

you but not to your spouse, you will need to devote more time and energy to neatness than you can reasonably require of someone who doesn't place neatness high on her list of priorities.

2. **Develop separate domains.** To the extent possible, if you and your spouse have widely different standards of order, carve out separate territory for yourselves. For example, one husband of an ADD wife despaired when he arrived home each evening to be greeted by clutter and chaos in the kitchen. The kitchen served as his wife's office as well as the kitchen. The counters and breakfast area, as well as her desk in the breakfast area, were filled with by piles of papers and unfinished projects. The couple were able to reach a compromise that worked well for both. The ADD wife agreed to establish an office and "project room" in the spare bedroom and to keep her papers and clutter out of the common areas of the house.

3. **When possible, hire a third party to do tasks that are difficult for your ADD spouse and that overburden you.** Too many couples get caught up in "ought to's." We shouldn't have to hire someone. She or he ought to be able to do this! A more practical approach can eliminate some of the prickles from your marriage. Try to move away from an attitude of judgment toward a realistic assessment of yourself and your spouse. Not everyone has the same energy level or efficiency. Some people need more "down time" than others. If there are chores that you and your spouse argue over repeatedly, perhaps there is a way to eliminate it from your life, either by simplifying your life or by hiring someone to do the task.

4. **Take a look at your own perfectionism.** Are you locked into the role of overfunctioning? Have you become overfocused on order, responsibility, and "ought to's" in reaction to your spouse's ADD? It may work best to try to meet each other in the middle.

Solving Problems Together

Sit down together and draw up a master list of regular household responsibilities. A sample list might include some of the following items. Depending upon your household, add to or subtract from this sample list.

Child-related tasks
Carpooling
Helping children with morning routines

Setting appointments
School meetings
Helping with homework
Supervising bedtime preparation
Attending sports events and school activities
Purchasing clothing, school supplies, athletic goods

Food-related tasks
Meal planning
Food purchasing
Meal preparation
Kitchen cleaning

Laundry
Collecting
Washing
Drying
Folding
Ironing
Putting away
Depositing and picking up dry cleaning

Household chores
Daily: straightening up, sorting mail, watering plants, dumping trash
Weekly: vacuuming, dusting, cleaning floors and bathrooms
Periodically: cleaning oven, refrigerator, closets, garage, windows;
responsibility for hiring and supervising cleaning of carpets, drapes,
etc.

Pet care
Feeding pet or supervising child who feeds pet
Walking dog or supervising child who walks dog
Training
Cleaning up after pet
Visiting veterinarian
Arranging for pet care when family is away

Yard maintenance
Mowing
Fertilizing
Watering
Mulching

Trimming
Planting

Household maintenance and repairs
Painting
Carpentry
Installation of lights, shelving
Minor plumbing and electricity
Caulking

Financial tasks
Long-term planning and financial management
Balancing checkbook
Paying bills
Shopping for health, auto, homeowner's insurance
Tax preparation and related record keeping

Automobile maintenance and repair
Filling with gas
Checking tires
Changing oil
Washing
Scheduling repairs

Are Your Commitments and Responsibilities Realistic?

The preceding list may seem lengthy and detailed; in reality, though, it is only a brief outline of household chores within a family. I have made it intentionally detailed in order to help you consider commitments more realistically. Many "ADD families" are overcommitted and feel frequently overwhelmed by a level of fatigue and disorder in their lives. In addition to improved time management and organization, these families also need to learn to cut back on complications and commitments in their lives.

Be realistic about yourself and your personal situation. Don't allow yourself and your spouse to be misled by what you see in non-ADD families or by what you think "you ought" to be able to accomplish. One young ADD couple made this mistake with disastrous results. They lived in a town house and had one child. Despite the wife's angry complaints about her husband's procrastination and lack of initiative at home, the coupe went ahead with plans to move to a larger home and have a second child.

The wife denied her husband's ADD, and he was reluctant to set firm limits on the responsibilities he could manage. This couple's mutual inability to accept the husband's ADD ultimately created much greater problems. As the family's responsibilities and stress level increased, the husband's disorganization, procrastination, and feelings of being overwhelmed grew in proportion. He felt chronically anxious and inadequate, while his wife responded with growing anger and dissatisfaction. Unlike this young couple, the first and most important task for you and your spouse to achieve is to *reduce* your family "to do" list to more manageable proportions.

Establish an "ADD-Wise" Division of Duties and Responsibilities

Once you have reduced your chore list, assign approximate time allocations to each task, and then begin to work on a division of tasks that makes the most sense given each of your strengths, weaknesses, preferences, and available time. Establish a plan in writing and make an appointment to review your plan in two weeks to assess how it is working. Dual-career couples will need to plan for work conflicts, especially if one or both travels on business. Reviewing this list may be an eye-opening experience for you both. You may decide that you need to cut back on commitments as you calculate the hours needed to complete these tasks. Writing everything down also makes both partners more aware of the many concrete tasks involved in managing a household.

As you look at each task, ask yourselves:

1. Given our schedules, which one has time to do it?

2. Which one of us likes to do it?

3. Which one of us is best suited to do it?

4. Is this something we should eliminate from our list by changing our lifestyle or by hiring someone else to do it?

Don't expect immediate perfection. Work toward becoming cooperative partners. Try to work with your partner to divide duties and responsibilities along the lines of your strengths, abilities, and interests. An ADD adult may find it tedious and frustrating to balance the checkbook monthly but may be very good at performing more physically active roles around the house. Because absentmindedness is often a problem for adults with ADD, routine tasks—

occurring each day at the same time—may be more appropriate because they become easier to remember. For example, taking the children to day care, or washing the dishes each evening, may be easier to remember than more irregular tasks such as scheduling the family's dental appointments or picking up an item at the store on the way home from work. For the same reason, tasks that can be done "right now" may be better than those that require planning and remembering.

EMOTIONAL OVERREACTIONS

Many adults with ADD have a tendency toward emotional overreaction. They may react intensely to other drivers who "cut them off," to traffic jams, or to other of life's many challenges and frustrations. At home, these overreactions may be in response to noise, disorder, a defiant child, or to a spouse who is once again upset that they are late for dinner and forgot to pick up milk on the way home from work. Medication, both stimulants and antidepressants, can often help control irritability and intense emotional responses. But medication alone cannot completely regulate the hyper-responsivity of the adult with ADD. Changes in interpersonal patterns and approaches to life management are essential, too.

1. **Eliminate stressors whenever possible.** For example, one man who worked in sales arranged his day so that he returned home before rush hour. He made his final phone calls and completed his paperwork in the quiet comfort of his home. Because he generally found crowds highly stressful, he planned his time for shopping on week nights and almost never on weekends.

2. **"Own" your overreactions; don't blame them on your spouse or kids.** Your irritability is not just hard on you but on those around you. Unfortunately, many adults with ADD tend to save up the irritations of the day and unleash them in the safety of the home environment. Instead of yelling at the boss or at a co-worker, the ADD adult yells at the first unlucky family member who crosses his or her path. If you arrive home tired and grumpy, establish a time for mental refueling, if possible. One man who found this hard to do at home developed a pattern of stopping by the library for a few quiet minutes before arriving home to his lively household.

3. **Apologize when your anger and irritation get the best of you.** Outbursts are hard to live with, but they are more tolerable when you admit you are in the wrong.

4. **Try to stop arguments or discussions before they erupt into explosions.** If you feel your anger rising, tell your spouse that you need to stop and cool off. But don't let this become a technique for avoiding problem solving. Promise your spouse you'll come back and talk when you're calmer. Then do it!

PROBLEMS WITH FINANCIAL MANAGEMENT

Many adults with ADD have difficulty managing their money well. This has to do with a number of ADD traits. ADD impulsivity may lead to many unplanned and unaffordable purchases. Poor planning—of meals, for example—may lead to wasting money on frequent carry-out or restaurant meals. Inattention to details may lead to little or no budgeting of expenses. Difficulty with paperwork may cause bills to be lost or to be paid late. Poor financial record keeping can result in delayed or never completed tax returns. In some extreme cases, adults with ADD have ended in bankruptcy, not because of inadequate income or life crises, but due to chronic overspending on hundreds of small items over the years, or failure to plan for retirement or institute an investment or savings plan. Money management and spending habits can become a source of anger and arguments within a marriage. Typical budgeting and financial management plans often don't work for ADD adults because they require too much disciplined, detailed record keeping—just exactly those skills that are lacking and that led to financial difficulties in the first place. Although it may work best for the non-ADD spouse to keep records and write checks to pay bills, it is normally not a good idea to have the non-ADD spouse be keeper of the purse strings. This imbalance, like others that may develop in ADD marriages, will eventually result in resentment on both sides. If you are an ADD adult who experiences great difficulty in living within a reasonable budget, here are a few things you might try:

1. **Remove yourself from temptation.** If you are an impulse buyer, don't use window shopping or "going to the mall" as a recreational activity. Make a list of needed items, look for sales in the paper, shop by phone—when possible for the best buy—and then make your purchase.

2. **Delay the impulse.** If you are shopping and find an item not on your list that tempts you, don't buy it at that moment. Go home, consider the purchase, and then go back to buy it if it is just too good to resist. Many ADD adults find that impulse purchases that are out of sight are also out of mind.

3. **Credit cards.** If you tend to make credit card purchases of items you can't afford at the moment, don't carry your card with you. Keep one card for emergencies.

4. **Walking-around money.** Decide with your spouse what is a reasonable sum of money for each of you to spend on incidentals each week, including lunches, snacks, soft drinks, magazines, and small incidental purchases. Withdraw that amount of money once a week and budget yourself throughout the week. Often Friday is a good day to draw your money for the week because more expenditures are likely to occur on weekends. Then, stay away from the ATM machine until next Friday!

Using these techniques will put you in charge of controlling your own spending impulses and will allow you and your spouse to relate in a healthier way as adult partners.

Coming to Terms with ADD as a Couple

We have discussed many potential problem areas in marriage for adults with ADD. It's essential, however, not to become so embroiled in focusing on the negative effects of ADD that you lose sight of the positive.

Keep Things in Perspective

Blanket statements such as "I can't count on you!" are all too easy to make and can create tremendous resentment and lack of trust. What the non-ADD spouse often means when making such a statement is "Your absentmindedness makes you forget things all the time, and that makes life really hard for me!" When you define the problem concretely—"your absentmindedness"—rather than using a blanket condemnation—"I can't count on you!"—you are on your way to finding solutions to the problem.

Create an "ADD-Friendly" Home

1. Don't choose a home or home furnishings that require meticulous upkeep.

2. Create "ADD space," in which clutter and chaos is acceptable, while setting aside common areas that everyone will work to maintain more neatly.

3. Learn to laugh together at minor ADD dilemmas.

4. Emphasize the positive things you have together and work toward making them a larger part of your life.

5. Make sure you have positive, nonjudgmental, time together each day.

6. Always look for ways to eliminate problems rather than harping on them.

By trying some of the approaches suggested here, and by taking this on as a challenge that you will meet together, you can work toward making your marriage a positive, supportive partnership.

6

Family Life:
Stresses and Strategies

Family Life:
Stresses and Strategies

W hen ADD affects one family member, it affects all members of the family. Because ADD can be passed down from one generation to the next,
a family with an ADD parent is likely to have one or more children with ADD.
Ned Hallowell, a noted psychiatrist who specializes in ADD, writes that families with ADD members need to accept ADD issues as facts of life that have
both a positive and negative impact on the whole family. The family needs to
learn as a group to understand and recognize ADD patterns, such as overreaction or argumentativeness, and to learn how to negotiate well—parent to parent,
parent to child, and sibling to sibling. Hallowell describes the tendency toward
arguments and explosions as "the big struggle" with which each family with
ADD must learn to cope.

THE ADD ADULT AS PARENT

First, let's look at parenting from the point of view of a parent with ADD. Then
we will briefly discuss some of the challenges of parenting a child with ADD.
Of course, these issues overlap and interact, but it may become more clear if we
consider them separately.

Consistency

For parents with ADD, consistent parenting can seem a monumental challenge. Consistency requires energy, which an ADD parent may not have at the end of a long day. Consistency also requires self-control. Many ADD parents find that they struggle constantly with a tendency to overreact to minor stressors when they are overstressed themselves. At other times, they may ignore a child's misbehavior because they are fatigued and tempted to take the path of least resistance. Consistency, especially in parenting children with ADD, is terribly important. While, at times, it may be tempting to ignore misbehavior, the long-term cost of inconsistent parenting is enormous, resulting in more defiance, more testing of limits, and longer tantrums.

Co-Parenting with Your Spouse

If you are a parent with ADD who is parenting an ADD child, more than likely, you need to make an especially great effort to work as a team with your spouse. If you and your spouse are at odds about which behaviors are acceptable or unacceptable, active teamwork is even more important. Consistent co-parenting will lead to a calmer household and fewer crises. It may be very helpful to work with an ADD specialist for a period of time to understand how your own ADD affects your parenting style, to learn effective parenting techniques, and to better understand what behaviors can be reasonably expected of children, especially ADD children, at various ages.

SPECIAL STRESSES FOR WOMEN WITH ADD

ADD homemakers (usually women) have particularly difficult roles. The job of mother and housewife is one of the most challenging because of its built-in lack of structure. Many women diagnosed with ADD report that they were able to perform well in the workplace but found themselves falling apart at home, especially following the birth of a second or even third child, when the demands for time management and organization increase tremendously.

Stress and irritability increase as the number of interruptions and daily crises increase. On the job, some women are able to shut their office doors, or at least focus on one thing at a time, with minimal interruption. At home they are awakened frequently at night, constantly interrupted while talking on the phone, and called to respond to crying children while trying to make out a grocery list. Typically the family stress on a mother with ADD tends to be greater than the family stress on a father with ADD. Even in these "liberated" times, traditional roles persist in most families to a greater or lesser extent, placing primary responsibility for children and household on the mother.

Raising Children with ADD

All of the struggles faced by adults with ADD pertain to children with ADD as well. They are prone to intense reactions, struggles with self-control, and inconsistent behavior. Parents with ADD who have ADD children can play a very powerful and constructive role by teaching them to understand the "family ADD" and by teaching them techniques for minimizing the struggles caused by ADD.

Establish Quiet Times

Quiet times—to be away from stress, to be alone, and to relax—are a very crucial self-management tool for both adults and children with ADD. Parents can teach this coping strategy to children. One ADD mother reported that, from toddlerhood, she taught her ADD daughter that "Mommy needs quiet time" and that "quiet time" was good for her daughter as well. She taught her little girl to listen quietly to music when stressed or upset and also taught her to leave her mother alone for a few quiet minutes periodically throughout the day. This mother told a humorous story of becoming frustrated by some minor crisis in the kitchen and being asked by her three-year-old if she needed some "quiet time." This daughter had learned a valuable lesson at an early age.

As children grow older, according to Kate Kelly and Peggy Ramundo, both ADD experts, quiet zones within the house need to be established. These are areas where no loud voices, music, or television will be heard, allowing family members peace and quiet when they need it. Try to think about noise and traffic patterns when you choose a home. It will make this process much easier.

Homes with basements or playrooms and with doors that can be closed off allow for more peaceful cohabitation with family members.

Establish Routines

Routines are essential for good functioning of an ADD home. After routines become firmly established, they are much easier to maintain. Routines can reduce the number of debates and degree of confusion over issues such as meals, homework, and bedtime. If there are few routines in your family, don't try to suddenly impose several. Choose one important area, and work for several weeks to establish a consistent routine before moving on to establish another.

Bedtime Routine

Chronic sleep deprivation can wreak havoc in an ADD family. Many children and adults with ADD tend to be night owls who have difficulty winding down at night to sleep. If these patterns are not overcome, both parents and children often are chronically sleep-deprived, which leads to more frequent tears, anger, and confusion. ADD parents who are successful in establishing a bedtime routine for children do themselves and their children an invaluable turn. Well-rested children are capable of more self-control the next day. Establish a pattern for children to go to bed early and then play or read quietly. This gives children time to wind down without cutting into their sleep time. Parents whose children go to bed reasonably early have time to relax and unwind, which allows them to be more patient and consistent parents the next day. Too many ADD parents report that they never have time to themselves or time to be alone with their spouse because they have never established consistent bedtime routines.

Mealtime Routine

Mealtimes, especially dinner, can be one of the most challenging times of the day for a family with several ADD members. Dinnertime is typically a time of fatigue for the whole family and a time of maximum competition for attention between family members. It is also, unfortunately, often a time to battle over what children refuse to eat and a time to argue over table manners. Children with ADD may be at their most irritable and restless. It is important that parents recognize their own limits, as well as the limits of their children, to prevent mealtimes from becoming free-for-alls.

Guidelines for Mealtimes

1. Don't try to use mealtime as a time to chat with your spouse. Build in a time before or after dinner as couple time. Kids with ADD have enough trouble sitting at the table without being expected to sit quietly while parents talk to one another.

2. Keep the mealtime short. Allow children to excuse themselves from the table when they have finished eating.

3. Have a "no-interrupt" rule, and remind each other in a friendly fashion when the rule is broken.

4. Likewise, set a reasonable time limit on monologues. Mealtime is a time for sharing, not monopolizing.

5. Teach kids to take turns talking.

6. Look for ways to make mealtimes pleasant. Talk together about upcoming family plans for the weekend.

7. Be flexible. Let a child or parent who has had a particularly rough day opt to eat alone.

8. Try to avoid struggles with kids over what they *must* eat. Save your battles for the important things.

Pick Your Battles Carefully!

A common mistake made by many parents of children with ADD is to become suddenly ambitious about making changes. Suddenly they want to establish rules and routines and to reward or punish their child for ten different behaviors simultaneously. This *never* works; and no matter how hard you try, the system you set up will *never* last! It may be very true that you can list ten problem behavior patterns that you would like for your child to change; but targeting all of them, or even half of them, without setting priorities makes it unlikely that any of them will really change.

Create your own list of ten problem behaviors, and then rank them in importance. Although each parent must do his or her own ranking according to his or her values, as well as the child's own behavior problems, some general guidelines are that physical violence, lying, disrespect, and direct disobedience are more destructive to family functioning than issues such as arguing over the television, not finishing vegetables, leaving a bike in the driveway, or having a messy bedroom.

Establish Rules and Consequences

Talk to your child, together with your spouse, when your mood is calm. Tell your child that you are unhappy about the way things are going at home and that you want to set up some house rules. Don't just set up punishments. Rewards are powerful tools in molding the behavior of children with ADD. Rewards don't have to involve treats or expenditure of extra money. Rewards can be something that the child already has and enjoys such as TV time, telephone time, a friend on Friday night, renting a video, or even a ride to soccer practice. In other words, let your children know that in order to continue to receive the goods and services they have been enjoying, they will need to be cooperative.

Don't expect perfection at once, though. Punishment should be swift and certain. In other words, don't warn your child, such as saying that "one more time" you'll have to go to your room. Tell your child in advance that disrespectful talk will result in "time out" in his room. Then enforce the "time out" immediately after the first infraction.

Don't threaten punishments you cannot or will not enforce. Many parents become so frustrated by defiant behavior that a punishment of half an hour of "time out" soon escalates to "All right, you'll have to spend the next week in your room!" When tempers have cooled, the punishment is canceled, and the child has learned only that parents can't be relied on to carry through with punishments. On the other hand, it's not a good idea to keep your child in her room for a week just because you made a threat in a heated moment! Try to keep your head, and make your punishments reasonable. If you impulsively threaten something you later reconsider, apologize, tell your child you have reconsidered, and then let him know what the more reasonable punishment will be.

If you are prone to impulsivity and to losing control yourself, it may be helpful to do some advanced planning with your spouse about reasonable rewards and punishments so that you are prepared to stay in control during the heat of the moment.

OVERREACTION AND THE RISK OF ABUSE

Many ADD adults are prone to intense reaction to frustration as are, of course, many ADD children. The combination can be problematic and, in extreme situations, dangerous. One ADD father of an ADD adolescent boy reported that he found he had to use every ounce of self-control to leave the room rather than engage in physical combat with his very provoking son. An ADD mother of young children found that her greatest problem arose after their prolonged temper tantrums or whining. She felt an overwhelming need to escape from the noise; and yet when she tried to distance herself from her preschoolers, their cries became louder as they followed their mother around the house. At times, she feared that her responses bordered on physical abuse when she was alone with her children for extended periods. Both of these parents needed to temporarily remove themselves from the volatile situation, but the young mother had less opportunity to do so.

What Can Be Done to Avoid Potentially Abusive Overreactions to Children?

1. Remove yourself from the scene immediately, if possible.

2. Engage the assistance of the other parent immediately, if possible.

3. If you are an ADD parent, home alone with children, try to build in a back-up system—a friend or neighbor nearby who can come over and defuse the situation.

4. With very young children, too young to place in "time out" alone, a change of situation will often defuse their tantrum. Try taking your screaming toddler for a ride in the car or a walk around the block to distract him or her.

5. Recognize your limits. Build in "down-time" for yourself. ADD mothers of young children may need to arrange for more babysitting or more time at preschool.

6. Problem solve with your spouse. During calmer times, talk together to develop consistent ways of responding to arguments, defiance, and tantrums from children.

7. Work with a child ADD specialist who can help you to develop more effective tactics to defuse potentially explosive situations.

Overidentifying with an ADD Child

How Can an ADD Parent Avoid Doing This?

Overidentification with a child who has ADD can sometimes interfere with good parenting. Sometimes this occurs when an ADD parent is fearful of the structure and discipline necessary for children with ADD because of the mistaken belief that this might be harmful to the child. When a parent's own insecurities, low self-esteem, and unhappy memories of childhood prevent him or her from exercising needed controls, then not only does the child suffer, but the household can suffer as well.

One mother with ADD and learning disabilities had experienced much unhappiness as a shy, awkward child in grade school. She overidentified with her own shy ADD daughter. Rather than helping her daughter learn to cope with insecurities at school, she opted to protect her through home schooling. Several years later, the daughter had fallen far behind academically and had learned no social skills to help her cope in the outside world. Through the best of intentions this mother had created even greater problems for her daughter!

School and Your ADD Child

How Can I Help My Child Avoid the School Problems I Experienced as an ADD Child?

There is more and more help available today for children with ADD. Your son or daughter should have a much easier time in school than you did. A generation ago, little was known about ADD in children. Today, although we have far to go, there is much more teacher training and much more information available about the educational needs of children with ADD.

Become actively involved in ADD organizations, and become an active member of your child's school. If your child continues to experience school problems after he or she has been diagnosed and is in treatment, you may need to contact an educational consultant who is an expert in ADD issues. Many children with ADD, especially in the higher grades (middle and high school), have great difficulty coping with the complexity and organizational demands of a large public school.

Homework Struggles with ADD Children

As an ADD parent, you may not be the best person to help your ADD child with his or her homework. Many ADD parents report that they become extremely frustrated when trying to help their children. Efforts that begin in a friendly fashion may soon deteriorate into angry battles. Homework typically takes an ADD child much longer to do than a child without ADD. After the school day, children with ADD are tired, bored, and impatient. Allow your ADD child time to be physically active after school. Then establish a homework routine that suits your child and household. Be consistent. Establish a routine of homework before allowing television, games, computers, or talking on the phone.

If homework problems are severe, your child may need a private tutor. You may also need to consider the possibility that your child may have learning difficulties in addition to ADD. Learning disabilities are very common among children with ADD.

SELF-ESTEEM AND YOUR ADD CHILD

How Can I Help My ADD Child to Feel Good About Himself?

The most damaging effect of ADD on a child is not necessarily caused by the actual difficulties in concentrating, remembering, controlling impulses, and achieving academically. Usually the greatest damage done to a child by ADD is a result of negative feedback from adults. "You dummy!" "How many times do

I have to tell you?" "For God's sake, stop that!" "You're just lazy." "You're just not trying." "You could do it if you wanted to." "Your forgetting is very convenient. You don't forget to go out to play!"

Sadly, many adults with ADD have not come to terms with their own difficulties. When they see the same problems developing in one of their children, they may react with even greater negativity instead of with understanding, as if being very strict, or very angry at ADD behavior, will eliminate that behavior in the child.

The best way to arm a child to cope with his or her ADD is to give him or her self-understanding, combined with self-esteem. Help your child look for activities in which to excel. Look for ways to eliminate struggles at home. Help your child to understand his ADD and to learn ways to compensate for it.

Establish "Special Times" with Your ADD Child

In the day of a child with ADD, there are many occasions for criticism and rebuke. What is essential for parents of children with ADD is to make sure there are also occasions each day for support, enjoyment, and sharing. Even fifteen minutes a day can make a huge difference in your relationship with your child and in his feelings about himself as a loved, worthwhile human being. "Special time" should be a time to spend on an activity chosen by the child and enjoyed by the child and parent together. This is not a time for teaching, correcting, or competing but simply a time to feel positive about being together. Let your child know that this time is special for you, too. Don't use it for leverage. In other words, don't tell your child, "Finish your homework, or no 'special time' tonight." Special time is not a reward but a time for building and strengthening relationships between parent and child. For older children, a good "special time" is after the younger siblings have gone to bed. This allows him or her to have your full attention without competing for it.

PARENTING AN ADD ADOLESCENT

Many of the symptoms of ADD are also typical of adolescents in general: impulsivity, disorganization, defiance, stubbornness, and emotionality. For this reason, in adolescence, ADD becomes A²DD! Many parents despair as their

ADD adolescent continues irresponsible behavior patterns after non-ADD peers begin to show signs of maturity.

Be realistic about what your adolescent with ADD can reasonably be expected to do. For example, because details and paperwork pose difficulties, even for adults with ADD, your adolescent is likely to need much assistance filling out forms, choosing colleges, or completing college applications.

Try to avoid head-to-head confrontations with your ADD teen. A very confrontational approach is more likely to increase conflict than to eliminate it. An extreme "tough love" approach has the potential for dangerous consequences. These teens are ill-equipped to survive outside the family support system, yet their defiance and impulsivity may lead them to desperate extremes. Look for less extreme measures than "You can't live here unless...." Boundaries are important, but they should be ones that can be safely imposed.

Be supportive and patient. ADD teens will grow up, but usually it takes several years longer to reach the same maturity level as a non-ADD young adult. Help them build skills and feelings of competence. As the parent of an ADD teen, you need to look for a middle ground between throwing your child into the deep end of the pool to sink or swim and rescuing that child immediately so that there is no possibility of ever learning to swim.

When a Parent Denies a Child's ADD

Sometimes a parent is in denial about a child's ADD symptoms because he is in denial about similar symptoms in himself. This was true for one father who was divorced from the mother of his ADD son. At his mother's house the child took stimulant medication and lived according to orderly routines. When he visited his father, however, the father refused to give the child medication and left him largely unsupervised. The father, although undiagnosed, manifested many ADD symptoms. Yet he believed there was "nothing wrong" with his son, just as there was "nothing wrong" with himself!

In some families, denial of ADD is so strong that there is little that can be done. In most families, however, the problem is the result of lack of information or misinformation. Some parents have read very negative information about medications used to treat ADD and feel adamant about not giving such medication to their child. Other parents simply know little about ADD or other learning problems and think that they are just new fads to be ignored.

Education is the best approach. Don't try to argue or insist. Ask your spouse to accompany you as you educate yourself about the learning and behavioral problems associated with ADD. Find a pediatrician who is expert in ADD, and set up a meeting with yourself and your spouse. Set up a school conference with your child's teacher. Ask your spouse to attend an ADD support group meeting with you.

PARENT TRAINING

Even non-ADD parents need parent training to learn to be effective with ADD offspring! These kids are particularly challenging, and many of the techniques that work with other children are simply not effective to control the behavior of ADD kids. As an ADD parent, you have a double set of challenges to face. There are many excellent books that have been written for parents of ADD children, some of which are listed in the Resource List. Educate yourself and your spouse through reading books, attending courses, and seeking ADD parent counseling. It may be one of the best investments you can make to improve your family life.

JOIN ADD ORGANIZATIONS

Excellent support is available for parents of ADD children through a number of organizations. Two of the largest are CH.A.D.D. (Children and Adults with Attention Deficit Disorder) and ADDA (Attention Deficit Disorder Association). Addresses and phone numbers for both of these organizations are included in the Resource List. There are local chapters in hundreds of communities across the United States. These organizations can offer not only parent education, but also the opportunity to talk with and learn from other parents of ADD children.

ADD FAMILY GUIDELINES

1. Don't sweat the little things.

2. Emphasize the positive.

3. Help your child find areas in which he or she can excel.

4. Look for ways to eliminate daily hassles.

5. Look for creative solutions.

6. Be consistent—hard in the short run but a big payoff in the long run.

7. Look for ways to eliminate stress in the family

8. Take breaks when you need them.

9. Get parent training and family counseling—work as a team with your spouse, build each other up, and bail each other out!

10. Talk with other parents of ADD children regularly—parents of non-ADD children really DON'T understand what you go through!

11. Look for ways to have fun as a family.

7

Improving Social Skills

Improving Social Skills

S ome ADD adults are very gifted interpersonally, and they find their talent for engaging people in conversation and in forming friendships to be one of their greatest gifts. These ADD adults are often drawn to sales, public relations, and politics, using their prodigious energy and interpersonal skills to great advantage. Many adults with ADD, however, find that the world of interpersonal relationships is a world that they traverse without benefit of a road map, wandering in a fog of missed cues, faux pas, and misunderstandings. This chapter will focus on difficulties that adults with ADD may experience in interpersonal relationships, offering some approaches for improving social skills.

John Ratey, a noted ADD expert, points out that the interpersonal difficulties experienced by many adults with ADD have neurobiological underpinnings. He writes that dysregulated neurotransmitter systems in the frontal lobes cause difficulties in impulse control as well as distractibility and with accurate minute-to-minute processing and interpreting of information. Appropriate interpersonal behavior depends on frontal-lobe inhibition (not saying the first thing that occurs to you), inhibiting the impulse to speak while someone else is speaking, accurately perceiving and processing subtle social cues, and developing a complex set of interpersonal cues and guidelines. Adults with ADD can experience difficulties in each of these areas.

Additionally, many adults with ADD report a difficulty in maintaining interest in relationships over the long term. They are very prone to become caught up in interests of the moment, rarely stopping to stay in touch with current or old friends. Some adults have such difficulty in maintaining relationships that they have fleeting friendships and multiple marriages, moving on once the initial interest has waned. However, John Ratey writes that the majority of adults with ADD are not fickle and put much effort and concern into relationships, only to find themselves repeatedly "making a mess of things." Low self-esteem, frustration, and poor social skills can lead some adults with ADD to retreat into a safer, but isolated, existence.

PROBLEMATIC INTERPERSONAL BEHAVIOR

Let's look at some of the typically problematic interpersonal behaviors seen in some adults with ADD as well as some tools for lessening the negative impact of these types of behaviors.

Interrupting

Interrupting is a very common ADD habit, a result of impulsivity and also of poor memory. Many adults with ADD report that they interrupt because they suddenly think of something they want to say and fear that they will forget their idea while waiting for the speaker to finish.

Coping Techniques

In our adult ADD support group we try to enforce a no-interrupting rule, using several techniques. One is to provide friendly reminders that an individual has interrupted. The other is to suggest that people keep pen and paper with them to write brief reminders if they have a question or comment.

Monologuing

Many adults with ADD are prone to give long monologues, talking "at" instead of "to" people. This is typically caused by "tunneling" or "hyper-focusing." Once they are interested in a topic or activity, they become totally engrossed and have difficulty shifting to another one. If an ADD adult has become hyper-focused on his topic, he is much less likely to attend to nonverbal social cues from his listener that may indicate waning interest.

One woman married to a man with ADD related that sadly she had come to avoid conversations with her husband. She felt lonely and craved real sharing with her husband. The problem arose from his prolonged monologues. He tended to talk endlessly on topics that held no interest for his wife.

The art of conversation requires skills opposite to those of the hyper-focused monologuer. Skilled conversation requires flexible shifting of conversational topics in response to subtle reactions from your conversational partner. It requires eye contact and ongoing attention to the other person's verbal and nonverbal responses that indicate whether the topic should be continued or changed. Skilled conversation is like an intricate tango, while the ADD monologuer marches straight ahead, expecting his audience to pay rapt attention from the sidelines.

Coping Techniques

1. **Look for the right audience.** If you are fascinated by computer technology, look for another "computer nerd" to talk to. Don't just pounce on the first person who passes by.

2. **Try to catch yourself when you've gone on for too long.** Train yourself to look for cues from the person to whom you are speaking. People who are simply nodding politely and making few comments are probably simply being polite. If your audience is nodding, smiling, or asking numerous questions, you've probably found the right audience!

Non Sequiturs

Some adults with ADD are prone to make completely extraneous comments from "left field." Sometimes the ADD adult has become bored with the ongoing conversation and has begun daydreaming. Often, however, this is not the case. A non sequitur may result from some odd association the ADD adult may make to the topic at hand. Non sequiturs can also result from internal distractibility. Even when interested in a conversation, adults with ADD report that their mind bounces from topic to topic despite their best efforts to remain focused. In rejoining the conversation after a foray into random thoughts, the ADD adult may make a comment that is so unconnected to the general conversation that associates may simply look askance or politely inquire about the connection between the comment and the conversation.

Coping Techniques

1. **Be an active listener.** Look the other speaker in the eye, nod to indicate interest, and make comments or ask questions related to what the speaker has just said. Active listening will help guard against distractibility.

2. **Guide the conversation.** Try to tactfully introduce a topic that interests you if you are uninterested in the current topic. Don't just passively allow the conversation to continue while you tune out.

3. **Apologize with humor.** When your wandering mind gets the best of you, comment on it humorously, "Don't mind me. I've just got too many brain cells firing at once!," and tune back into the ongoing conversation.

Distractibility

Many adults with ADD are highly distractible. Sights and sounds around them uncontrollably draw their attention away from the person to whom they are speaking. Such looking away might indicate lack of interest in a person who doesn't have ADD. As an adult with ADD who is highly distractible, you don't want to give your friend or colleague the misimpression that you are uninterested.

Coping Techniques

1. Look for quiet places to talk.

2. Explain to the other person that you are having difficulty concentrating; don't leave them with the impression that you are uninterested in what they are saying.

3. In restaurants, try to choose a table away from the action. Choose a seat that faces away from the room and toward your conversation partner.

4. When possible, at home or at work, close the door.

Bluntness

Bluntness can be thought of as the opposite of diplomacy. A diplomatic statement is carefully couched in terms designed to cause the least offense. Bluntness, on the other hand, results from saying the first thing that comes to mind without considering the possible consequences. In some circumstances bluntness can even be an asset. Some hard-driving business people with ADD may use bluntness to their advantage in certain types of negotiations. If adults with ADD can learn to moderate their bluntness to a degree, they may be appreciated for their "tell it like it is" approach.

Unfortunately, for some ADD adults, their bluntness just offends those around them, leading people to assume that the ADD adult either doesn't care about the feelings of others or, worse, has offended them intentionally. This is rarely the case. Many ADD adults report with chagrin that they put their foot in their mouth repeatedly without meaning to. It's as if the words just leap out before they have an opportunity to catch themselves.

Coping Techniques

1. Try to slow yourself down as you talk. Consciously try to give yourself time to think, especially if the topic is a sensitive one.

2. You are more prone to speak without careful thought when you are excited or emotional. In an argument or dispute where your feelings are running high, it may help to develop the habit of excusing yourself temporarily from the conversation or suggesting that it be continued at a later time.

3. Do some advanced planning when you have to speak to someone about a sensitive issue. Actually write down words and phrases that you plan to use.

4. Get some feedback from a spouse or close friend if you anticipate a difficult conversation with someone. Ask for suggestions about more diplomatic ways to discuss potentially hurtful topics.

Hypersensitivity to Criticism

Ironically, although some ADD adults can be insensitive to their own effect on others, they are often, at the same time, hypersensitive to criticism or negative feedback. This hypersensitivity results both from an internal, physiological tendency to overreact emotionally and from what has often been a lifetime of criticism for their ADD behaviors. This hypersensitivity can make open, honest communication quite difficult. Sometimes, no matter how gently a suggestion or comment is made, the adult with ADD responds with anger, denial, and defensiveness. The fine-tuning and adjustment needed in all relationships, whether in work life or personal life, become extremely difficult if your friend or colleague receives an extreme reaction from you in response to even the mildest complaint or criticism.

Coping Techniques

1. Develop an awareness of your "overreactions." Recognize what you are doing and try to moderate your reactions when you feel they are occurring. Use self-talk, such as "I'm really upset, but I realize it's probably an overreaction."

2. Try to anticipate situations in which you may overreact. Rehearse ways to speak and react in advance if you anticipate a difficult meeting or encounter.

3. If you have overreacted, leave the scene if possible, and come back later to talk to your friend or colleague after you have had a chance to calm down.

4. With very close friends and colleagues, it may even be appropriate to explain to them that you realize you are overreacting and would like to talk to them later when you are feeling more calm.

5. Get feedback from someone you trust if you feel unsure whether your feelings about a certain conversation or situation are appropriate or exaggerated.

Missing Social Cues

Often people with ADD are so caught up in their own thoughts or feelings that they may overlook important social cues without realizing it. An adult with ADD may become caught up in proving a point in a discussion, while completely overlooking the fact that the person he is talking to is tired, bored, or offended. This can also happen when leaving a social situation. Adults with ADD may repeatedly think of "one last thing" to say, overlooking the fact that their hosts have been patiently standing at the door for several minutes anticipating their imminent departure.

Coping Techniques

1. Practice reading social cues as you watch people. It may never become second nature to you, but it is a skill you can improve on.

2. Make active choices to interact and socialize, as much as possible, with people who are more direct, and therefore easier to "read."

3. Ask for help from a close friend or spouse: "Just kick me under the table if I keep going too long." "Say something to me when it's time to leave."

Poor Listening Skills

Listening skills are difficult for many adults with ADD. Ability to stay tuned-in may vary with the topic, but the majority of adults with ADD find that they tune out when listening to lectures, discussions, or even prolonged personal conversations. Their listening ability is worse when they are stressed, tired, or uninterested. Some people also find that listening is more difficult when they feel they are required to sit still without any activity or movement. Close friendships and intimate relationships cannot be built and maintained if your friends or spouse feel that you "never really listen."

Coping Techniques

1. If listening for an extended period feels overwhelming to you, try to explain this to your friend or spouse. Briefer conversations in which you are truly involved are far better than half-listening to a longer conversation while a friend tries to communicate something important.

2. Experiment with holding and manipulating some small object while you listen. Some adults find that even this minimal activity helps them stay engaged.

3. Try talking as you go for a walk. Physical activity may enhance your ability to stay tuned-in.

4. Practice playback techniques in conversation. Listen and then repeat in your own words what you've understood the other person to say. "You mean...?" This kind of active listening will help keep you engaged.

5. Monitor your own internal state. Don't try to converse when tired, hungry, stressed, or otherwise distracted.

Preoccupation

Some ADD adults unintentionally ignore others because they are "lost in their own world," preoccupied with some issue they are pondering, or some problem they are solving. These "absentminded professor" types are more common and more accepted in some work and social environments than in others. Preoccupation can take a toll on close relationships, however, if your spouse, roommate, or close friend never quite feels he or she has all of your attention. In the workplace, preoccupation can cause unintended offense if you repeatedly walk past co-workers without acknowledging them or are so lost in your own thoughts that you don't respond when spoken to.

Coping Techniques

1. Close friendships and intimate relationships need time and attention if they are to be sustained. Actively look for times of day or activities that will minimize your preoccupation, allowing you to be present to your spouse or friend.

2. Try to develop the habit of pulling yourself "out of the fog" several times during the workday to briefly interact and acknowledge others. Constant preoccupation gives co-workers the message that they are unimportant.

3. Take time to say "Good morning" to co-workers before diving into your work.

4. Some adults with ADD become nearly "deaf" when hyper-focusing on something. Even when someone calls their name, they may not hear. Explain to people that you get lost in your own thoughts and that they may need to tap you on the shoulder when you don't answer. Assure them that you are not ignoring them purposely.

Wearing Other People Out

ADDers of the more hyperactive type may cause difficulties in relationships by wearing out the people around them. Adults who have ADD with hyperactivity (AD/HD) often need less sleep, have more energy, talk more, and want to go go go all the time. Such people can be very stimulating and exciting, but they may exhaust partners, friends, and colleagues after a certain point has been reached.

Coping Techniques

1. Spread yourself more thinly. You may need to interact with more people in order not to overwhelm any one of them.

2. Pay attention when people tell you that you are "too much." Even too much of a good thing can wear out a relationship.

3. Look for other high-energy people to be around.

4. Pay attention to social cues. You may not be ready to call it a night, but if everyone else is, don't pressure them to keep going.

Interpersonal Impatience

If you are an ADD adult on the hyperactive end of the continuum, you may damage relationships with others through obvious impatience. Some adults with ADD describe that they feel as if most of the world is in slow motion. It is difficult for them to wait for people to finish their sentences, make decisions, or accelerate when the traffic light changes. If impatience is paired with insensitivity, such an ADD adult may come across like a bulldozer, trying to push people to "get to the point." ADD adults who are on fast-forward may be prone to harass family and co-workers with their impatience. "What's taking so long?" "Let's go. I don't have all day!"

Coping Techniques

1. Try to accommodate your own needs without pressuring others. If you want to leave sooner, take your own car.

2. If you hate to be kept waiting, give your companions a departure time a few minutes in advance. That way, even with dawdling and inevitable delays, you won't be kept waiting too long.

3. Try always to bring something with you to read or to work on.

4. Back up and take a few slow breaths. Because you want people to do everything more quickly won't make it happen. All that you'll accomplish is to offend and harass the people you're trying to rush.

5. Get regular exercise. Often a sense of perpetual impatience is made worse by pent-up energy.

Disappearing Acts

Do people you're close to tell you things like "I never know where you are."; "I never know when you'll be home."; "Half the time you're not where you say you'll be."; "I call you, but you're never there." Relating to some people with

ADD is a little bit like trying to hold on to quicksilver. Now you see them. Now you don't. These kinds of behavior patterns are partially due to hyperactivity and impulsivity but are also a result of not thinking about the needs of those you're close to. These patterns can be extremely destructive in a marriage or other close relationship.

Coping Techniques

1. Keep in touch. Keep in touch. Keep in touch. If it's hard for people in your life to reach you, make sure that you make an effort to reach them.

2. It's OK to change your plans. Just be sure that you consistently let people know what the changes are and how to reach you.

3. Make yourself more accessible by using a beeper or car phone.

4. Keep a joint calendar with your spouse or significant other. Make sure that all your plans and commitments are written on the joint calendar.

5. Don't let your poor time management continually steal time from important relationships. Go home, spend time with the important people in your life, and then finish your work later in the evening if you need to.

CREATE AN "ADD-FRIENDLY" INTERPERSONAL ENVIRONMENT

Ned Hallowell, co-author of *Driven to Distraction,* and noted ADD expert, is an adult with ADD himself. He writes from his own experience as well as the experience of countless adults he has treated in his psychiatric practice. Dr. Hallowell advises adults with ADD not to linger long where they are not appreciated. By this he does not mean that ADD adults should run impatiently and impulsively from one person to the next but to look for people, in your personal life as well as your work life, who can really appreciate the positive things you offer and who are not hypersensitive or easily bothered by your ADD traits. Work toward creating an ADD-friendly interpersonal environment for yourself. This can happen through good choice of friends. Many ADD adults find that they are most comfortable with other ADD adults. They are on the same wavelength and can tease and laugh about each other's foibles in an accepting manner. You can also create an ADD-friendly environment by addressing your ADD traits in a more relaxed and open manner. "If I keep interrupting you, just tell me to keep quiet! I try my best, but sometimes my mouth engages before my brain does." Such a humorous apology eases the tension for everyone and makes others aware that you are trying your best to be considerate of them.

This chapter has focused on a number of interpersonal problem areas for some adults with ADD. If you recognize any of your own patterns on this list, don't let yourself overemphasize the negative. Recognizing problems is a huge step toward solving them. You may need support and feedback as you try to develop some of the suggested coping techniques. It may be helpful to try counseling or group therapy as a way to get feedback and focus on developing social skills. And, remember, social skills aren't developed overnight. Expect to be repeatedly catching yourself doing the "same old thing" as you work toward developing new habits.

Most important, keep a hopeful attitude. Learn about your interpersonal patterns, recognize problem areas, and consistently work toward bringing about changes that can make future relationships much more satisfying than they may have been in the past. Learn to appreciate your positive traits, and look for others who appreciate them as well.

8

ADD in the Workplace

ADD in the Workplace

Through luck or intuition, some adults with ADD are enormously successful in their careers. For many others, however, their ADD struggles seem to be most evident on the job because often it is our work that places the greatest demands on our capacity for planning, memory, organization, teamwork, and precision. Many adults with ADD have chosen their careers haphazardly. As they encounter difficulty or dissatisfaction on the job, they may suddenly leave, only to take another position with little planning or forethought. Some may leave jobs out of boredom, others because of poor working relationships, and still others because they are not able to meet the demands of the job. As a result, it is not unusual for ADD adults to have a checkered résumé reflecting a pattern of job hopping.

A different pattern can be found among some adults with ADD who have excellent career records until they are eventually promoted to a management position. At that stage the demands for time management, planning, and organization become too great and their job performance suffers. Sadly, other adults with ADD are chronic underachievers. They may have intelligence and talent; yet their inconsistent level of motivation, their disorganization, or tendency to procrastinate has led them to job assignments far below their real capacity. Despite high intelligence, many have not completed a college degree; others have reached the level of graduate or professional school but were unable to complete their degrees. In sum, for many ADD adults, work life has been far from ideal, resulting in chronic feelings of discouragement and dissatisfaction.

This chapter focuses on ways to avoid these troubling ADD career patterns. The following sections will address:

1. Techniques to successfully cope with ADD patterns on the job

2. How your employer can accommodate your ADD

3. Protection provided to adults with ADD by the Americans with Disabilities Act

4. Disclosing your ADD to your employer and educating your employer about ADD

5. Ways to find a good job match if you have ADD

6. How to learn the "success traits" found in highly successful individuals with ADD and become a proactive self-advocate at work

Managing ADD Patterns at Work

This section lists some typical ADD patterns in the workplace and offers practical suggestions for coping with or reducing them. Some of the techniques may not be applicable to your particular work situation but may stimulate ideas that you can modify to better suit your own needs.

Hyperactivity/Motor Restlessness

Adults with ADD of the hyperactive/impulsive type are often drawn to jobs that allow them freedom of movement throughout the day, perhaps as a salesperson who follows a route or as a self-employed person who goes from one job to the next. Some ADD adults are not overtly hyperactive but experience intense restlessness when they sit at their desks for prolonged periods. Here are some coping techniques that may reduce problems with hyperactivity.

1. Look for work that allows a high degree of physical movement.

2. If your job requires prolonged desk work, take frequent breaks. A quick walk to the water fountain, or even a longer walk down the block and back, can reduce restless feelings and allow you to continue working.

3. Bring your lunch to work so you can spend your lunch hour exercising or going for a walk.

4. The more sedentary your job, the more important it is to regularly exercise either before or after work.

5. Carry a small, unobtrusive object in your purse or pocket that you can handle when sitting in long conferences or meetings. (Be sure to choose something that will not distract those around you.)

6. In meetings, always carry a pad and take notes. Even the small degree of movement involved in writing can help contain restlessness.

Distractibility

Unfortunately, the modern workplace environment places workers in the midst of multiple distractions. Just like the open-classroom experiment a generation ago, which proved disastrous for children with ADD, the open work space environment, which provides only cubicles and which places many employees within earshot of each other, presents a great challenge to adults with ADD.

1. When possible, arrange your work day to provide blocks of uninterrupted time.

2. Route phone calls to voice mail. Pick them up and return phone calls during specific time blocks. Don't allow phone calls to randomly interrupt your work throughout the day.

3. If you have a private office, shut your door for certain periods throughout the day.

4. If you don't have a private office, look for unused space—perhaps a conference room—where you can go to work on projects that require maximum concentration.

5. Experiment with earplugs, sound-screen machines, and headphones to reduce distracting noises in the workplace.

6. Utilize flex-time to provide yourself with an hour at the beginning or end of the day when fewer people are around to distract you.

7. Keep your work surface clean and clear. Visual distractions caused by piles of clutter tend to reduce productivity.

Internal Distractibility

For some adults with ADD, their biggest struggle is with internal distractions rather than the sights and sounds around them. Many ADD adults are prone to daydream when bored. Others are blessed with a rapid flow of ideas, which is a tremendous asset when managed well but can become a chronic distraction from the work at hand if poorly managed.

1. Daydreaming may be more likely if you have set aside too long a block of time to work on a particular task. You may find yourself more productive if you assign time-limited blocks to each task. Experiment and observe yourself to learn your maximum period of efficient functioning.

2. If you daydream frequently despite your best efforts to stay on task, you may need to seriously review whether your job is a good match for you. Some adults with ADD who see themselves as ineffective in one job can become highly productive when they switch to a job that really engages their strengths and interests.

3. When you are distracted by ideas that come to you in the process of work, develop the habit of writing them down in a specified place (not a random scrap of paper but a folder or notebook set aside for this purpose). This assures that you won't forget your idea and allows you to continue with your current task. These ideas can be very valuable but are destructive if they continually take you off task.

4. Similarly, in meetings, take brief notes about comments you want to make. This will keep you from rambling and help you to communicate in a more succinct, effective fashion.

5. Poor follow-through on projects is often a result of distractibility. The adult with ADD is interrupted, becomes caught up in a new task or idea, and forgets to return and complete the initial task. Adults with ADD need to train themselves to "tie the bow" on each project before allowing themselves to leap forward to the next thing that has caught their interest.

Organization

If organizing long, multistep projects is one of your downfalls, you may find some of the following ideas to be helpful.

1. Look for a more organized co-worker to team up with on long projects. Such partnerships can be highly productive when the ADD "idea person" is teamed with someone who may be less imaginative but better at administrative tasks.

2. Develop the habit of setting aside 15 minutes at the beginning of each work day to review both immediate tasks and long-term projects. Estimate and assign approximate times for each task. Set a priority list and plan your day accordingly.

3. Look for a job that entails more immediate problem solving and short-term tasks.

4. Try to avoid jobs in which you are assigned to work with several groups or are assigned work by several different people. Such positions can be difficult even for persons with good organizational skills.

Time Management

Adults with ADD are known for their difficulties with time management! They often lack an awareness of the passage of time, especially when involved in activities that interest them. They are typically poor at estimating how long a given task will take and tend to overcrowd their schedule. Many adults with ADD are chronically late because they try to squeeze in "one more thing" before departing for a scheduled event. Developing time-management skills can solve a multitude of problems caused by ADD patterns.

1. Learn to think proactively rather than reactively. Plan your day and follow your plan. Don't let your day run you by reacting moment-to-moment to events, moods, or impulses.

2. Don't overschedule your day. Learn to *overestimate* how long things will take.

3. Leave time for the unexpected.

4. Keep your day planner with you at all times—to refer to, to add to, and to revise as you need to throughout your day.

5. When you make a commitment to do something, don't just add the task to a huge, undifferentiated "to do" list. Assign an *actual time* on an *actual day* to complete that task.

6. To combat a tendency to lose track of time, set a beeper to go off five minutes before you need to leave for a scheduled event. Some day planner computer programs have built-in reminders.

7. Develop the habit of saying, "I'd like to, but let me check my schedule," rather than saying "yes" to a request without considering your previous commitments.

8. Avoid last-minute impulses unless they are true emergencies. Squeezing in "one last thing" before leaving leads to chronic lateness, giving others the unintended message that they are unimportant to you.

9. Plan to be early. Take a book or something to work on while you wait for the scheduled event to begin.

10. Begin phone calls by setting a time limit. "I need to leave for a meeting in ten minutes but wanted to catch you before I left."

Procrastination

Procrastination can present a lifetime struggle for many adults with ADD—it may be the result of disliking certain tasks, but it can also result from not knowing where or how to begin. If you procrastinate constantly on the job, you may need to seriously think about finding a job that interests you more. Procrastination on a particular task may simply be an indication that you need a little assistance or consultation in order to get started.

1. Give yourself deadlines. You'll get more accomplished.

2. Ask your supervisor for a deadline. Tell him or her that deadlines are helpful to you. Some supervisors believe they are doing you a favor by saying, "Just get it to me when you can." For an ADD procrastinator, such a comment is the "kiss of death." *Anytime* tends to become *never.*

3. When facing a boring or tedious task, build in small rewards to keep yourself going. "I'll take a coffee break as soon as I finish this memo."

4. Work on a team with someone else. When someone is counting on you to do a certain portion of a project, you will be more likely to complete it.

5. Look for work that involves short-term tasks with definite deadlines.

Low Frustration Tolerance

Low frustration tolerance is an inborn trait for many adults with ADD. Nevertheless, there are many things you can do to decrease frustration level if you take a proactive stance. This is an important issue to work on. High levels of chronic frustration not only take a toll on you, but also on those around you.

1. Try to pinpoint recurring events at work that are the most frustrating for you. Look for ways to reduce the frequency of these events.

2. Don't wait until you reach your "boiling point" before removing yourself from a frustrating situation at work. An inappropriate explosion at work can cause long-term damage to working relationships.

3. Try to avoid working for intense, high-pressure organizations.

4. Learn and practice relaxation techniques that you can use throughout the day at work as your stress level builds. A number of techniques involving imagery, muscle relaxation, and deep breathing are brief, effective, and can easily be done at work.

5. Look for work that allows you more autonomy to set your own hours and work pace.

Interpersonal Conflicts at Work

Some adults with ADD have such strong needs for independence and autonomy that they are better suited to self-employment. Although there has been very little research on workplace issues for ADD adults, some preliminary surveys indicate that the rate of self-employed professionals and entrepreneurs is much higher among the adult ADD population than among the general population.

Other ADD adults find that they need the structure provided by a workplace environment. And many types of work simply cannot be done without the support of a company or corporation. For these reasons, most adults cannot opt for self-employment; as a result they need to identify and work on patterns that may cause interpersonal problems at work.

1. If you have a history of difficulty with supervisors or co-workers, it is essential that you analyze and understand your own contribution to those difficulties. Feedback from a trusted friend or counseling may be helpful.

2. Some adults with ADD "don't know when to stop." They may keep on and on at something, missing important nonverbal cues that they are angering their boss or co-worker.

3. Some ADDers are prone to be stubborn or argumentative. They need to recognize these patterns and work on learning flexibility and compromise.

4. If you are prone to be hot-tempered or explosive, it is important to closely monitor your frustration level and learn to remove yourself temporarily from the frustrating situation before an explosion occurs.

5. If you find that you are impatient with others who operate at a slower pace, or who may make mistakes that seem "stupid" to you, you may not be well suited to positions requiring you to supervise others.

6. Even within a large organization there are jobs that allow more independence and autonomy than others. If you find that working closely with others leads to great frustration, it may be important to look for a more autonomous position.

7. Many ADD adults dislike close supervision, especially if the supervisor tends to be a bit controlling, detail oriented, or critical. If you are experiencing chronic difficulty with your current supervisor, it may be wise to actively seek reassignment to a supervisor who is more compatible with your personality.

(For more information on solving interpersonal problems at work, refer back to Chapter 7.)

Memory

Although memory difficulties have been given little attention by ADD researchers, adults with ADD almost universally report that they tend to be forgetful and absentminded. The more complex and multifaceted the job, the more memory difficulties may interfere with good performance.

1. Use tape recorders or take extensive notes at meetings and conferences.

2. Take your day planner with you always so that you can refer to events and tasks of the day.

3. Use your day planner as a constant reminder pad. Many day planners

provide a page for taking notes opposite the page on which the scheduled events of the day are listed. By writing a note there you not only have a record of what was said, but also the day on which the commitment was made.

4. Keep a written record of all requests you make of co-workers, as well as of all requests that are made of you.

5. Ask people to send you information by fax or E-mail. That way, you automatically have a written record.

6. Use a computer version of a day planner (there are numerous programs available) that has a built-in reminder feature.

7. Develop the habit of placing objects that you intend to take to work near the door of your house, and place near the door of your office or cubicle those things that you intend to take home with you.

8. No matter how simple, don't rely on memory. Write yourself notes on sticky pads and place the notes in clear view. Some find it helpful to place notes on the telephone or on the computer screen so that they cannot be overlooked.

9. Develop the habit of reviewing your day, as well as the upcoming week and month, to remind yourself of upcoming commitments and events.

Ways Employers Can Accommodate ADD

You have just considered a long list of coping skills and strategies that the adult with ADD may find useful to counteract problematic ADD patterns at work. There are also a number of things that can reasonably be provided by your employer that may greatly improve your ability to function on the job. The Americans with Disabilities Act (ADA) requires employers to make "reasonable accommodations" for employees with disabilities. This chapter lists accommodations that might be considered "reasonable" for an employer to provide to individuals with ADD. Some of these accommodations are taken from a list published by the Job Accommodations Network. (See the Resource List for address.) Others are ideas that have developed from counseling adults with ADD about problems in the workplace.

1. Provide, wherever possible, a nondistracting work space.

2. Allow the employee to do some of his or her work at home when it does not interfere with other aspects of the job.

3. Provide the employee with computer software to assist with planning and time-management tasks. Software that provides visual or auditory reminders is most helpful.

4. Provide the employee with audiotape equipment to tape meetings and conferences.

5. Provide the employee with checklists to structure multistage tasks.

6. Give instructions slowly and clearly.

7. Provide a written version of instructions for future reference.

8. Excuse the employee from nonessential tasks, allowing him or her to better focus on essential tasks.

9. Restructure the job, if necessary, to better match the employee's strengths.

10. Provide more frequent performance appraisals.

11. Reassign the employee to a vacant position that better suits him or her.

12. Provide extra clerical support.

13. Allow flex-time so that the employee can do more work during periods of the day that are less distracting.

14. Establish frequent, brief regular meetings with his or her supervisor to assist the employee in keeping on task. Some communication can even take place in writing in order to avoid excessive supervisory time.

15. Establish multiple short-term deadlines.

16. Provide assistance in setting up an organized filing system.

17. Communicate as much as possible by memos and E-mail.

18. When work assignments come from multiple sources, provide assistance in setting priorities.

Americans with Disabilities Act (ADA)

What Are Your Rights Under the ADA?

Attention Deficit Disorder qualifies as a disability under the ADA if it can be shown that it substantially impairs your ability to function in the workplace. If you can meet the standards of a job, and meet the requirements of that job with reasonable efforts on your part and reasonable accommodations on your employer's part, then the employer is required by the ADA to provide accommodations for ADD. No legal cases have yet set standards for what accommodations are deemed "reasonable" under the Americans with Disabilities Act. These standards will be set in courts of law as various individuals with ADD elect to file suit against their employers for failure to provide reasonable accommodations.

The concept of "job requirement" goes beyond a literal job description. An individual must have met the academic requirements as well as required on-the-job experience. In addition, not only must he or she be able to perform specific tasks required by the job, but he or she must also meet general standards of cooperativeness such as coming to work on time, obtaining permission for any absences during the day, and meeting the required number of work hours.

What constitutes a "reasonable" accommodation also depends on the size and circumstances of the employer. Generally speaking, the smaller an employer the fewer accommodations would be required because they might place an undue financial burden on the employer. The ADA only applies to organizations with greater than 15 employees.

DISCLOSING YOUR ADD AT WORK

The decision of whether or not to disclose your ADD on the job is a personal one that must be based on your particular circumstances. It is quite possible to request certain accommodations without disclosing an ADD diagnosis. Often, if an employee demonstrates a good work attitude and high motivation, a supervisor will make efforts to accommodate problems wherever possible without the disclosure of a disability. For example, one woman who worked as an administrative assistant explained to her boss that she found the front office very distracting, especially when she needed to concentrate on a particularly demanding task. She was given permission to use her boss's office when the boss was away several times a week. This accommodation occurred without any disclosure of ADD.

Another individual, a computer specialist with ADD, told his supervisor that he found it very draining and unproductive to attend some of the meetings each week that he was normally expected to attend. He suggested that he would have an easier time meeting an upcoming deadline if he could be excused from certain meetings in order to focus on his work. Because this man was a hard worker who had a good relationship with his supervisor, they were able to agree on a plan that eliminated wasteful meeting time. Again, this accommodation was made informally, without disclosure of an ADD diagnosis.

It is usually best to try to find solutions and accommodations in an informal, cooperative fashion, without disclosure of ADD whenever this is possible. It is difficult to predict the results of disclosing your ADD. Most employers know little about ADD, especially in adults. Incorrect assumptions could be made based on your disclosure.

There are times when disclosure is necessary, however. Typically these include situations that cannot be resolved informally. When you have failed to obtain reasonable accommodations on an informal basis, and find that you are unable to perform your job adequately without those accommodations, disclosure may be in order. Likewise, when you fear you are in danger of being fired or demoted because you need accommodations in order to perform your job, disclosure is in order.

If you do decide to disclose your disability, it is also your responsibility to inform your employer about what types of accommodations you will require. You may need to consult with someone who is expert in ADD issues in the workplace in order to develop a list of accommodations to request. You may find it helpful to refer to the accommodations listed in this chapter as a starting point in developing your own customized list.

EDUCATING YOUR EMPLOYER ABOUT ADD

Because the awareness of ADD in adults is so new, few employers have experience in working with ADD employees. You may find that you are breaking new ground in your particular place of work if you choose to disclose your ADD. In order for your disclosure to be beneficial, your employer needs to become knowledgeable about ADD and supportive of your efforts.

You might begin by setting up a meeting with your supervisor to talk about the specific ways that ADD affects your job performance. This meeting would be an appropriate time to make suggestions about accommodations and also to brainstorm with your supervisor about possible ways to accommodate your needs in your particular work environment. It is important to emphasize that you plan to take primary responsibility for managing your ADD problems. Let your supervisor know of the steps you are taking to improve problems with organization, time management, or distractibility. Ask him or her for suggestions and regular feedback on your progress.

Some adults with ADD have even arranged meetings between the ADD expert with whom they are working and a representative of the organization for which they work in order to develop a plan for accommodations. If this is not possible, it may be helpful to suggest books on ADD in the workplace to your employer. (See the Resource List.)

Sometimes one of the most important accommodations on the job can be a change of supervisor. Supervisors who tend to be rigid, perfectionistic, micro-managers or overly critical are bad matches for adults with ADD. The ADA, however, does not require an employer to provide you with a supervisor to your liking! If you feel that you are not able to obtain a supportive work environment under your current supervisor you may need to look around for other positions, either in your current company or outside it.

Finding the Right Job Match

People with ADD often ask the question, "What are the best kinds of jobs for people with ADD?" Unfortunately there is no list of "ADD jobs." People with ADD are affected by it in different ways. In addition, people with ADD have different personality types, levels of intelligence, abilities, skills, and areas of interest. All of you, not just your ADD, needs to be considered when looking for the right job match. One thing is certain, however—finding a good job match is more important for adults with ADD than for the average person. Adults with ADD struggle continually with motivation problems, procrastination, boredom, and restlessness. The more interesting you find your job, the more successful you will be in challenging these ADD patterns.

If you are still in school, still considering a choice of career, or if you feel you have made an incompatible career choice and would like to make a change, here are some general guidelines that may be helpful to consider.

Develop a List of Strengths and Weaknesses

Think back over your life, considering summer jobs, courses in school, hobbies, and extracurricular activities. Make a list of strengths.

Similarly, think about things that have been very difficult and frustrating in your life. These might include courses in school as well as certain types of job activities.

Develop a List of Likes and Dislikes

Let your imagination roam as you work on this list. Include everything you can think of, whether it's immediately related to work or not. What things fascinate you? What bores you to tears? How much do you enjoy interacting with people versus engaging in solitary activities? What activity level do you prefer? Do you like to sit for hours in front of your computer, or are you happiest when hiking through the hills?

It may be helpful to take an interest inventory. These are tests designed to help people make a good career choice. Such tests compare your likes and dislikes against the interests of people who have been successful in various fields of endeavor. These tests won't recommend specific career paths, but will suggest a number of directions that seem to suit you best.

The Myers-Briggs Type Inventory

The Myers-Briggs Type Inventory (MBTI) is a questionnaire that has been developed to categorize people according to 16 different personality types. The MBTI can be a helpful tool in making career choices, used in combination with the rest of the information you have gathered and compiled about your strengths, weaknesses, likes, and dislikes. There have been many studies on the types of careers that typically interest people with various MBTI personality types.

DEVELOPING "SUCCESS TRAITS"

Individuals with learning disabilities who had achieved great success in their careers were studied by a researcher named Paul Gerber. Although LD and ADD are not synonymous, the LD and ADD factors that most affect workplace performance are very similar, making Dr. Gerber's findings highly relevant for adults with ADD. He found that individuals who achieved a high level of success in their careers despite their learning disabilities all reported the following internal traits:

1. A very strong desire to be successful

2. A high level of determination

3. A strong need to control their own destiny

4. An ability to reframe their disability in a more positive, productive manner

5. A planned and goal-oriented approach

6. An ability to appropriately seek assistance without becoming dependent

These successful people also reported a common set of external circumstances that they had been fortunate enough to find or resourceful enough to create for themselves:

1. A mentor for guidance and support

2. Positive, supportive people to work among

3. New work experiences to enhance their skills

4. A work environment in which help was available when needed

5. A high "goodness of fit" between their skills and the job's requirements

BECOME A PROACTIVE SELF-ADVOCATE ON THE JOB

You need to become an expert on yourself in the workplace. Although your employer can accommodate your ADD to a certain extent, the lion's share of responsibility for career success lies with you. You need to develop a very positive, proactive stance toward your worklife, learning to:

1. Realistically assess your ADD traits and how they affect your job performance.

2. Come to understand your interests and abilities.

3. Analyze your "workplace personality" and the circumstances and relationships that work best for you.

4. Work with your ADD rather than letting it work against you.

5. Actively develop ADD "success traits."

6. Actively seek an "ADD-friendly" work environment.

Don't expect instant change and immediate success. You may find that you can make a better job choice and work successfully toward changing patterns if you find a counselor or job coach who can help you keep on track. Don't expect to make career changes entirely on your own. Remember, the "success traits" found by Dr. Gerber include finding a mentor for guidance and asking for help when needed. Although it is true that many individuals with ADD experience difficulties in the workplace, it is just as true that individuals with ADD are highly successful in many fields of endeavor. Following the guidelines presented in this chapter should provide you with many tools to find a successful career track.

9

Continuing Your Education

Photo copyright © Sylvia Johnson

Continuing Your Education

If you were not diagnosed with ADD until adulthood, you have probably not had the opportunity to benefit from the great progress that has been made in accommodating the needs of students with ADD. Any school that receives federal funds (which basically includes all colleges and universities) is now required to provide accommodations for students with Attention Deficit Disorder. In addition to accommodations required by law, many schools also provide extensive support programs offering tutoring, specialized assistance with registration, classes in study skills and special courses designed to remediate areas of academic weakness. A number of books have been written for college-level ADD students that provide very useful tips and techniques. As a result of these advances, it has never been easier for students with ADD to succeed in school. If you have not completed your education or if you are contemplating a return to school for an advanced degree, you should become informed about services for which you may be eligible and strategies that will offer you the best chances for success in completing your degree.

RETURNING TO COLLEGE AS AN **ADD** ADULT

What Do You Need to Do?

Obtain Documentation of Your ADD

To be eligible for special services at a college or university, you must have recent documentation of your disability. Most schools prefer a psychological evaluation that includes IQ testing. Because many adults with ADD also have undiagnosed learning disabilities, it is a good idea to be evaluated by someone who is knowledgeable about learning disabilities as well as ADD. If you have a particular school in mind, contact the Disabled Student Services office (DSS) at that school and ask for the type of documentation they require.

Check for Accommodations for Qualifying Examinations

Accommodations are now available for students with ADD who must take entrance exams such as the SAT (the Scholastic Aptitude Test), the GRE (Graduate Record Examination), and all of the other standardized qualifying examinations. You can request extended time when taking these tests, and you can take them in a quiet, nondistracting place away from others taking the exam. Many people with ADD find that their scores improve significantly when they take such tests with accommodations.

You will need very specific documentation of your ADD. Because guidelines for such documentation have been in flux, it is a good idea to check directly with the organization that administers the test you must take, in order to make sure you have the specific documentation they require. Be sure to leave enough time. This process can take quite a few weeks to complete.

Look for a School with a Good Support Program

By law, all colleges and universities must provide accommodations for students with Attention Deficit Disorder. The services provided by different schools are not all the same, even though they may appear similar in the catalog. How can you make a good choice of school? Contact the DSS office in each school that you are considering, and ask the following questions:

1. Is the director of the office a specialist in LD or ADD?

2. If not, is there a full-time staff member in the DSS office who is a specialist in ADD or LD?

3. How long has there been a support program for LD or ADD at that school? (Generally speaking, programs are more comprehensive if they have been in place for a number of years.)

4. How many students are registered for LD/ADD services on campus?

5. Is there a physician on campus, or affiliated with the school, who has experience in prescribing medication for students with ADD?

6. Are there courses in study skills available for students with ADD?

7. Are ADD students given priority registration privileges?

8. Are specialized advisors available to students through the DSS office?

9. Are accommodations made for a reduced course load in all undergraduate and graduate programs?

A few guides are published each year that highlight colleges and universities recommended for students with special learning needs. Some of these are listed in the Resource List. It may also be useful to seek a college placement counselor who has specialized knowledge of schools and programs for students with ADD.

ACCOMMODATIONS FOR ADD STUDENTS

What Types Are Available?

Not all schools provide the same services. Below is a list of commonly provided accommodations:

1. Extended time on quizzes, tests, and exams

2. Provision of a quiet, nondistracting room in which to take tests

3. Note takers for your classes or access to the professor's notes

4. Permission to make audiotapes of classes

5. Reduced course load

6. Alternative test formats

7. Moderation of exam schedule to avoid two exams on the same day

8. Priority registration to assure you the schedule you need

To learn about how to succeed in college or graduate school with ADD, you should refer to more specialized books on the subject listed in the Resource List.

WILL I SUCCEED IN SCHOOL?

Don't let your past history of failure overshadow your desire to complete your education. Several factors are on your side as you return to school as an adult:

- Treatment for ADD will improve your concentration and follow-through.

- Accommodations are now available that will make your academic life easier.

- Greater maturity is on the side of the returning student: You are much less likely to be distracted by those things that were so appealing to an 18- or 20-year-old.

- You have more self-knowledge—about who you are and what you care about.

- You are in a better position to choose an appropriate course of study.

WHAT ELSE SHOULD I CONSIDER AS A RETURNING STUDENT?

Specialized Programs

Some students with ADD succeed better in alternative types of college programs. Some programs provide more hands-on experience. Others allow credit for life experiences of the returning student. Still others arrange course schedules differently—for example, allowing students to take only one course at a time, each lasting a few weeks. Some schools allow you to design your own curriculum and major. A few programs around the country allow you to do much of your work at home, traveling to campus periodically to meet with your professors. Many schools have programs designed for adults who work full-time, offering college courses at night.

Interactive Classes

Look for the types of classes that will keep you engaged. Large classes that allow little opportunity to ask questions or to become actively involved are classes in which you are more likely to lose your concentration. Smaller classes typically provide more opportunity to interact with your professor and fellow students.

Advocate for Yourself as an ADD Student

Work Closely with Your DSS Advisor

Most colleges and universities now have a DSS (Disabled Student Services) office. The more closely you work with the DSS office, the more likely you are to succeed in school. Your DSS counselor can assist you as problems arise, before they become overwhelming. Your counselor can also help intervene if you are having difficulty obtaining the accommodations you need in a particular class.

Inform Your Professors About Your ADD

Make a habit of requesting an appointment with each professor during the first week of each course. Let him or her know very directly what accommodations you will need. Some students are reluctant to disclose their ADD to their professors. Then when problems arise—after they have done poorly on an exam, for example—they seek accommodations from their professor. If you wait until problems arise, your ADD diagnosis can appear to be an "excuse."

Don't Assume Your Professor Knows How to Help You

Very few college professors have extensive knowledge or experience in working with students with ADD. You will need to be highly specific about your needs. One good way to do this is to provide each professor with a brief, clear written statement describing how you are affected by your ADD and what types of assistance you will need from your professor. It is best if such a statement is written on letterhead from the DSS office so that your professor knows that you are registered with that office and that the accommodations you seek are sanctioned by them.

Stay in Touch with Your Professors

When professors know that you are interested and involved in their courses, they are more likely to work with you in whatever way they can. If you are experiencing difficulty in a particular course, make an extra effort to talk to the professor often, seeking advice and assistance. Let him or her know you are working hard.

Actively Seek the Support You Need

You may need to find a tutor for especially challenging courses. Ask for tutor recommendations both from the DSS office and from your professor.

Join a Support Group on Campus

Many colleges have support groups for students with learning disabilities and Attention Deficit Disorder. These groups can be extremely helpful, not only by providing moral support, but also by providing you with valuable information regarding the best courses and teachers on campus.

"SUCCESS STRATEGIES" FOR ADD STUDENTS

Reduced Course Load

Students with ADD should routinely plan to take a reduced course load. Many students are tempted to take on too many courses or too many challenging courses at the same time. Often such students end up with a transcript liberally peppered with course withdrawals. This pattern is discouraging to you as a student and produces a transcript that gives a negative impression. It's much better to be realistic about the course load you can handle, and then work hard to make your best grades in these courses.

Audit First

If a course is required in a particular program of study that you anticipate being very difficult, audit the course before you take it for credit. That way the material is familiar to you. You will have read the text and heard all the lectures in advance. This may sound like a lot of trouble, but it's a lot better for your self-esteem and your transcript than failing the course and having to take it again anyway!

Tutoring

Don't wait until you're having trouble. In a course where you anticipate having difficulty, get a private tutor from the outset. It can even be helpful to work with a tutor prior to taking particularly challenging courses.

Summer School

Be careful about courses you sign up for in summer school. Many schools offer two summer sessions, each lasting about five or six weeks. Courses offered in these brief terms are very accelerated. Don't take a difficult course during one of these terms. If you are behind by only a few days, it can be hard to catch up.

WAYS TO IMPROVE STUDY CONCENTRATION

Some adults with ADD report that, even with the benefit of medication, they continue to find concentration difficult when they try to read or study for extended periods of time. If you are planning to return to school, it is essential that you be able to concentrate. Here are a few tips that may help:

- Choose high-interest courses whenever possible. Interest greatly enhances concentration.

- Experiment with studying in different environments. Some do best in a quiet room, studying alone. Others concentrate better when they play a radio to screen out extraneous sounds.

- Don't study in or near your bed if you are easily tempted to drift off to sleep.

- Be realistic about how long you should be able to concentrate. The more difficult and demanding the material, the shorter the time span for effective concentration.

- Move around while studying. Some college students with ADD find it helpful to walk around their room while reading. Jogging while listening to tapes of class lectures can also be an effective method of study.

- Read aloud to yourself when your concentration is beginning to flag.

- Study with others.

- Become an "active learner"—don't just read and underline. Use a micro-cassette recorder, and summarize each paragraph by dictating into the recorder. Listen to this synopsis of the material later while running or walking.

ALTERNATIVES TO A COLLEGE DEGREE

In spite of all the help that is available now to older, nontraditional college students, college still may not be the right choice. Many adults with ADD find that school is just not a good environment for them. The thought of taking many courses, including those that hold no interest for them, is completely unappealing.

If you feel this way, it may be better for you to consider training aimed more narrowly toward the development of specific job-related skills. Many programs at community colleges offer both Associate of Arts degrees and certificates in a number of career fields. In addition to degree or certificate programs, you may simply choose to take a number of courses, either at your community college or at a private, vocationally oriented school, to develop specific skills. These might include photography, computer skills, culinary skills, and automotive skills, for example.

Many adults with ADD are drawn toward owning and running their own businesses. The idea of being their own boss is very attractive. If this appeals to you, you may want to take specific courses—in accounting, business planning, or management skills, for example—without attempting to earn a formal business degree.

WHEN ADD INTERFERES WITH ON-THE-JOB LEARNING

As jobs become more complicated and more technical, on-the-job learning is increasingly common. Such learning may consist of information about new policies and procedures or learning more complicated processes such as new software systems.

ADD can have a huge impact on your ability to learn in such situations. Typically, training takes place in large groups and over many hours at a stretch. Neither of these practices is very "ADD-friendly."

What can be done under these circumstances?

If you have disclosed your ADD at work, you may be able to receive an accommodation allowing you to have additional training time or to have some one-on-one training or supervision following the standard group training.

Without disclosing your ADD, there may still be several helpful approaches to take:

1. Ask for permission to tape the training module. A videotape with an audio track is the most useful because it includes all information presented both visually and auditorily.

2. Take extensive notes; compare your notes with others to make sure that you have noted all the high points of the presentation.

3. Ask your supervisor for extra instruction following the presentation.

4. Take extra time to study, rehearse, practice—on your own time.

5. Use a laptop computer at home to work with new software systems until you have been able to master them.

6. Expect to devote extra time after hours to learning new systems or procedures.

7. Make yourself a set of outlines that briefly describe steps or procedures that you are learning to follow.

THIS IS THE BEST TIME!

There Has Never Been a Better Time for Adults with ADD to Study and Learn.

Many adults with ADD have understandably developed very negative feelings toward school. Often their ADD went unrecognized during school years. Without benefit of treatment and academic accommodations, school was a very frustrating and demoralizing process.

Returning to take courses after an ADD diagnosis, however, can be a very different, more positive experience. Medication often makes reading, concentrating, and remembering much easier. Additionally, as an adult, it is more likely that you are taking courses that are of interest to you or have a direct practical application for your career. Typically, it will be easier for you to concentrate on such courses because your interest and motivation is higher.

Learning to understand yourself, your ADD, and your learning style can greatly enhance your ability to study and learn. You may need testing for learning disabilities as well as an ADD diagnosis. You may need to work with a tutor who can teach you organizational skills as well as more efficient, effective ways to study.

All of these factors, taken together, mean that your chances for success are greatly improved! Numerous adults who were unable to complete college courses at age 18 or 20, before they received an ADD diagnosis, returned to school later when they were receiving treatment for ADD, taking medication, receiving accommodations, working with tutors, and making A's! With the right support you have an excellent chance to add your name to the growing number of adults

10

Women and ADD

Women and ADD

W hy is a chapter of this book dedicated to women and ADD? Why not one for men and ADD? The majority of writing and research on ADD has focused on males. Now, more and more women with ADD are being identified, a result of the recent recognition of ADD in adults as well as greater awareness of the "predominantly inattentive" subtype of ADD, which appears to be more common among women. Women with ADD struggle with a variety of issues that are different from those faced by men. This chapter will highlight some of those differences and talk about the struggles faced by women with ADD, both the "hyperactive-impulsive" and the "inattentive" type.

WOMEN VS. MEN AND ADD

Why Are Fewer Women Identified with ADD?

Statistics are still quoted suggesting that four out of every five children with AD/HD are boys. These statistics came from examining children who exhibited the ADD "holy trinity" of distractibility, impulsivity, and hyperactivity. Because girls are less likely to be hyperactive-impulsive, the high proportion of males, reported by these statistics, is not surprising. As the DSM-IV now recognizes the existence of ADD of a "predominantly inattentive type," so too are more girls being identified with ADD. As we begin to gather statistics on children who are both hyperactive and non-hyperactive, some speculate that the demographics of ADD will change to a more nearly even representation of males and females.

The early studies of adults suggested that ADD adults were predominantly male. However, these retrospective investigations focused only on adults who had been diagnosed in childhood with AD/HD. Because in the past the great majority of children diagnosed with ADD were hyperactive boys, these retrospective studies of adults were necessarily investigating a primarily male population. As adult ADD clinics have developed in a number of university settings, allowing the investigation of newly diagnosed adults, perhaps we will have the opportunity to study more women with ADD and to expand our knowledge of this overlooked group.

Other Reasons More Boys Have Been Identified with ADD

It has been observed that both parents and teachers tend to focus more on boys who are experiencing academic difficulties than on girls. Little girls who are more compliant and sit quietly at their desk unable to complete their work may be considered immature, passive, or as having less academic potential. Perhaps on some level, even in these "liberated times," both parents and teachers are more concerned about boys, who are expected to grow up and support a family, than about girls who, even today, grow up to work in lower-paid "service" professions that require fewer academic credentials.

It is also possible that, until recently, adult women with ADD were less likely to seek treatment. ADD at home is manifested in unfolded laundry, fast-food meals, mess, and disorganization. The consequences of these difficulties at home can go relatively unnoticed. The same inability to focus, plan, and follow through in the working world has more dramatic and more negative results. Men who have lost their jobs or who are chronically underemployed due to ADD symptoms may be much more likely to seek diagnosis and treatment.

Childhood Issues for Girls with ADD

Although the primary focus in this chapter is on the issues faced by women with ADD, it seems important to go back to childhood to trace the roots of some of the differences between boys and girls with ADD. Let's read the recollections of several women with ADD in childhood and adolescence, and then we will follow up with how these issues develop in adult years.

Typical Struggles for Inattentive Girls

Marie is an introverted, "primarily inattentive" woman with ADD who has struggled with anxiety and depression, in addition to ADD, both in childhood and adulthood.

> The thing I remember the most was always getting my feelings hurt. I was a lot happier when I played with just one friend. When someone teased me, I never knew how to defend myself. I remember whenever I was with a group of girls I always felt kind of overwhelmed and kind of out of it.
>
> I worried all the time because I didn't know what the teacher had told us to do, and I felt too embarrassed to ask anyone. I hated it when the teacher called on me because half the time I didn't even know what the question was. I really tried, but I remember one teacher who always made comments when I didn't know the answer. Sometimes I would get stomachaches and beg my mother to let me stay home from school.   —Marie, age 34

These recollections are very different from those of a typical AD/HD boy in elementary school. In fact, many parents or teachers would have simply assumed that this little girl was shy and had difficulty relating to other children. Her teacher might have assumed that she was preoccupied with emotional issues.

Her poignant recollections offer us clear illustrations of two problems frequently experienced by "primarily inattentive" girls. She was *hypersensitive to criticism,* had difficulty with the rapid give-and-take of group interactions, and felt socially "out of it" except in the company of her one best friend. Second, she was a compliant girl whose greatest desire was to *conform to teacher expectations* and not draw attention to herself. Her distractibility, which led to teacher disapproval and rebuke in front of her peers, also led to painful feelings of embarrassment and inferiority.

Some of the following traits are typical of non-hyperactive ADD girls:

Shy
Introverted
Easily embarrassed
Try hard to conform to teacher and parent expectations
Hypersensitive to criticism
Very reactive to stress
Nonassertive
Forgetful
Inefficient
Daydreamy

Typical Struggles for Hyperactive-Impulsive Girls

Shelly is a woman whose ADD is of the "hyperactive-impulsive" variety.

> I was always getting in trouble for something. In class I talked all the time. My teachers seemed to like me even though I had trouble getting my work done. I guess I learned how to act warm and cute and silly so that the teacher wouldn't get mad at me. I remember sitting in class in grade school, and everyone would get out their books and paper and start writing. I would just sit there feeling awful, wondering how everyone knew what they were supposed to do. I always had to ask the teacher what to do, but I tried to ask her in a way that she wouldn't get mad. Everybody liked me, but I guess they thought of me as really scatterbrained. Even now, as an adult, when I screw up by being late or forgetting, I go out of my way to do something for that person so they won't be mad at me.   —Shelly, age 38

Instead of jumping, climbing, and knocking things over, as some little AD/HD boys do, this girl's hyperactivity took the form of hyper-sociability. Unlike some AD/HD boys, though, she did not recollect anger or defiance. In fact, she worked extra hard to develop social skills to compensate for her distractibility and disorganization. She worked very hard to avoid negative reactions, although she was not always successful. Shelly was not identified by parents or teachers as having an attention problem, but rather was viewed as being scatterbrained and irresponsible.

Lauren's "hyperactive-impulsive" ADD patterns are most similar to those seen in many AD/HD boys. She was not only hyper-social, but physically hyperactive. She also recalls being stubborn, angry, defiant, and rebellious. Although we don't yet have adequate statistics for behavior patterns in ADD girls, it seems likely that women such as Lauren are in the minority when we examine female ADD patterns.

> I can remember in grade school that everything felt frantic. I could never get to sleep at night. I used to lie in my bed and listen to the radio or look at books or magazines. I was always exhausted in the morning. I felt like crying, and I hated to be rushed. Mom was always telling me to get dressed and get ready for school. I just wanted to go back to sleep. I had a fight with Mom almost every morning before I got to school.
>
> At school I was always jumping around, talking, and passing notes. Some of my teachers liked me, but some of them—like the really strict ones—didn't like me. And I hated them. I argued a lot and lost my temper when the teacher got mad at me. My desk was a huge mess. I remember sometimes that the teacher made me stay after school to clean out my desk.
>
> I remember that I still wet my pants when I was in second or third grade, and the other kids teased me. I cried really easily too, and some of the mean kids in the class liked to tease me and make me cry. Everything felt like such a struggle. The summers were wonderful. I could sleep as late as I wanted and didn't have to worry about school.
>
> —Lauren, age 27

Although we notice the argumentativeness and defiance in Lauren, which is seen more often in AD/HD boys, we also see that, like many ADD girls, she was hyper-social and hyper-emotional. Life for Lauren, as for some other girls with ADD, was an emotional roller coaster. She was very disorganized and had very low tolerance for stress.

Girls of the hyperactive-impulsive subtype may show some of the following traits:

Hyper-talkative
Hyper-social
Intense emotional reactions
Argumentative
Stubborn
Distractible
Disorganized
Poor self-control

ADD Adolescent Girls

Let's take a look at the recollections of Marie, Shelley, and Lauren about their adolescence. Life, for each of them, seemed to become even more difficult. Adolescence is difficult in general. When ADD is added to the mix, problems are amplified and stresses are intense.

> I hated high school. I was shy and incredibly self-conscious. High school just overwhelmed me. None of my teachers knew me because I never spoke up in class. Exams terrified me. I hated to study and write papers. They were really hard for me, and I put them off to the last minute. I didn't date at all in high school. People didn't dislike me, but I bet if I went back to a class reunion that no one would remember who I was. I had two good friends in high school. I tried to be with just one of them at a time. If we all three sat together at lunch, I felt left out and got my feelings hurt. I felt lost in high school. I was pretty emotional, and it got ten times worse just before my period. I usually fought with my sister or mother when I had PMS.
>
> —Marie, age 34

> If you asked people what I was like in high school they would probably tell you that I was really nice, really warm, and a total scatterbrain. I had a good time in high school, but my grades were terrible. I was always losing things or ruining things and then arguing with my parents about buying me new ones. One time I cleaned out my drawers and found five hairbrushes. I talked on the phone all the time when I was home and talked in class all the time when I was at school. I was a little wild but not too much. My father constantly lost his

temper because I left the lights on, because my room was a wreck, or because I hadn't done the dishes or something. He called me spoiled and irresponsible. Mom came to my rescue. I was always creating problems, and I got pretty good at talking my way out of them.

—Shelly, age 38

I was totally out of control in high school. I cringe when I think of some of the things I did. Because my grades were so bad, I tried to make up for it socially. I hung around with the popular crowd. Lots of partying, drinking. I was smart but a terrible student. My friends were smart, but they were good students. I guess I worked on being a "party animal" to make up for all the things I wasn't good at. Lots of my friends were cheerleaders or athletes. It seemed like I wasn't good at anything but hanging out with my friends.

I was sexually active from the time I was 15. I don't even like to think about some of the things I did. At home I was angry, totally rebellious. I snuck out of the house after my parents went to sleep at night. I lied all the time. My parents tried to control me or punish me, but nothing worked. I couldn't sleep at night and was exhausted all day in school. School meant nothing to me. My parents kept talking about the future, but that was just a word to me.

I had terrible PMS. Things were bad most of the time, but when I had PMS I really lost it. Sometimes my mom and I had terrible screaming fights. I would curse and yell. Once I even hit her. I feel terrible when I think back about what I was like.   —Lauren, age 27

Marie, Lauren, and Shelly present three different pictures during their teenage years. Marie was shy, withdrawn, a daydreamer, who was disorganized and felt overwhelmed. Lauren was hyperactive, hyperemotional, and lived her life in a high-stimulation, high-risk mode. Shelly's hyperactivity was more moderated. She worked hard at social skills to compensate for her impulsivity, forgetfulness, and disorganization. What do they show in common?

Severe premenstrual syndrome. In teenage years, the neurochemical problems caused by ADD are greatly compounded by hormonal fluctuations. These combined dysregulated systems result in enormous mood swings, hyper-irritability, and emotional overreaction.

Peer problems. Girls with ADD seem to suffer more as a result of peer problems than do boys with ADD. Although both Shelly and Lauren report that they had many friends in high school, both mention that they worked very hard to have such a social life. Their social life had very high priority for them, and ADD got in the way repeatedly.

Marie, by contrast, had difficulty keeping up with the rapid give-and-take of teenage-girl interactions. She felt overwhelmed, withdrew, and felt most comfortable in the company of one close friend.

Among hyperactive-impulsive girls—a sense of shame. Although usually this feeling of shame develops a few years later, studies of both men and women who have had a very impulsive, high-risk, immediate-gratification lifestyle during their adolescent and young adult years show that females tend to feel a great sense of shame once they have made a decision to give up that lifestyle. Males, on the other hand, feel neutral or even recall their former escapades humorously.

Adolescent boys who are impulsive and hyperactive may be viewed as simply "sowing their oats." They may even gain much peer approval as they rebel against authority or as a result of their hard drinking, fast driving, sexually active lifestyle. Girls with similar behavior tend to receive much more negative feedback from parents, teachers, and even from peers. Later, as women, many of them join the chorus of accusation and outrage, blaming themselves and feeling a strong sense of shame for such culturally disapproved behavior.

SPECIAL ISSUES FACED BY WOMEN WITH ADD

The preceding sections have focused on girls and adolescents with ADD. Now let's consider what type of issues are difficult for women with ADD.

Social Expectations

The Caretaker Role

For a woman with ADD her most painful challenge may be a struggle with her own overwhelming sense of inadequacy in fulfilling the roles she feels are expected by herself, her family, and society. Both on the job and at home, the great majority of women are expected to be caretakers. This means that, despite her own problems with planning and organization, a woman with ADD is expected to support, track, manage, and oversee the activities of others, both at home as wife and mother, and at work as nurse, secretary, teacher, or administrative assistant.

Many men with ADD are advised to build a support system around themselves—secretaries, wives, and subordinates—as an ADD coping mechanism. By contrast, not only do few women have access to such a support system, but society has traditionally expected women to *be* the support system for others.

Dual-Career Stresses

The struggles for women with ADD have been intensified with the emergence of "dual-career couples." More and more women have been required to not only fulfill most, if not all, of the more traditional roles of wife and mother, but also to function efficiently and tirelessly as they juggle the demands of a full-time career. Such a life requires constant shifting between the demands of the workplace and home.

While many men with ADD cope with the stresses of the workplace by hyper-focusing on career demands, women with ADD are forced into a more complicated juggling act involving home and the office. Additionally, many fewer women who work have a support staff in the workplace to assist in managing details and paperwork.

Single Parenting

Divorce rates are close to 50 percent among all marriages in the United States. Divorce may be even more likely when ADD is added to the list of marital stressors. Following divorce, it continues to be predominantly the mothers who are the primary parent for children. Compare the recollections of both a man with ADD and a woman with ADD who are divorced single parents.

Pat is a non-hyperactive woman with ADD who has been divorced for many years. She has two nearly grown children—a son with AD/HD and a daughter.

> I've just completely given up. I feel so exhausted when I come home from work. My son has been so rebellious, and his father is not here to back me up when we battle. He finally just dropped out of high school and has worked on and off—mostly off. Thank goodness I haven't had much trouble with my daughter. She's been pretty ma-

ture and is helping put herself through college. My son is so angry that I just try not to argue with him as much as possible. He keeps our house in a complete mess. I can't keep up with things, and I can't make him help. I haven't invited anyone over in years. I'd be so ashamed to let anyone see how I live. I am in therapy so that I can take charge of my life and get the strength to insist that my son move out.

Don, who also has ADD without hyperactivity, has a grown son who lives in another city. He recalls his relationship with him after his divorce:

After my divorce my son used to come visit. When he was with me, though, the only thing I could manage was taking care of him. I couldn't get anything else done, and my life fell apart, especially when he came for several weeks in the summer. I was relieved when he returned home. I couldn't handle taking care of him and keeping the rest of my life on track, too.

Both of these single parents with ADD have suffered as a result of their ADD, but their suffering was due to dramatically differing sets of circumstances. Societal pressure, role expectations, and the unwillingness of the father to play an active role in parenting all led Pat to live a live of stress, desperation, and total disorder. She felt she had lost her own life and fought years later to take possession of it again. Don, although he has experienced much sadness, opted for the traditionally male role of non-primary parent. He realized that his coping skills were not sufficient for single-parenting, and he declined that role. Pat never had that option.

A compromise between Pat's chaos and Don's isolation would probably have been better for each of them. A third single parent with ADD, Anne, found that compromise. She has ADD with hyperactivity and impulsivity and has experienced a roller-coaster existence all of her life. Her marriage ended in divorce after she had given birth to two children, one of whom has ADD. The children's father remained nearby and involved in their lives. Anne's parents also lived nearby and played very active roles as grandparents. As she explains:

Luckily, the children's father agreed to share custody with me. They were with him about half of the time. My parents helped out with after-school care. Things weren't always easy trying to co-parent with my ex-husband, but I couldn't manage at all if I didn't have his help. Therapy and medication helped me maintain control of my emotions and stay more focused. I learned better ways to manage my kids. I don't know what I would have done if I'd had to do it all myself.

This last scenario, with both divorced parents involved, along with a support system of grandparents and friends, is one that provides the happiest outcome for all concerned.

Unfortunately, in modern American society, most divorces end with women being expected to shoulder the main burden of single parenting. By adding ADD to the huge burden of single parenting, the result is often exhaustion and emotional depletion. Women with ADD need to learn that they have the right to ask for support as well as how to build a support system for themselves.

Physiological Differences: Hormonal Fluctuations

The hormonal fluctuations that commence at puberty continue to play a strong role in the lives of women with ADD. The problems they experience with ADD are exacerbated by their monthly hormonal fluctuations. Some women report that the stresses of being the primary parent of children with ADD, along with their own struggles with ADD, reach crisis proportions on a monthly basis during their premenstrual phase, often lasting as long as a week.

Marie, who is quiet, distractible, and non-hyperactive, describes her PMS as extremely painful:

> Sometimes I can hardly force myself out of bed when I have PMS. I feel exhausted, depressed, and teary. My son (who has ADD) doesn't know what's the matter with me. I don't have the energy to argue with him. Sometimes I just start crying when he gives me grief. I scream and lose my temper, which I don't usually do. I just feel like I can't manage the simplest thing. And I hate myself for being that way.

Marcie, the single mother of two children, is very hyperactive and impulsive. Here she describes her premenstrual phase in much more volatile and dramatic terms:

> There are times when I'm afraid I am going to commit child abuse when I have PMS. One of my sons is hyperactive. I have enough trouble handling him most of the time, but when I have PMS I get so

angry at him that I scare not just him, but myself, too. Sometimes I just can't take it, and I call my mother or a girlfriend to come over, just to keep me from going crazy or overreacting to the kids. It's so hard to keep myself going with my ADD. When you add PMS, it's just more than I can take. My doctor has given me antidepressants to take to manage my PMS. They help, but it's still pretty bad.

Marriage for Women with ADD

Escape into Marriage?

Some women who were later diagnosed with ADD recalled that their survival mechanism in young adulthood was to "escape" into marriage. They had struggled with school, were working at very low-paying jobs, and were having a tough time learning how to become self-sufficient and to manage their lives independently. These women married at a time when most women assumed they would "stay home with the kids." They "escaped into marriage," fearing that they would not be able to cope well with the demands of the workplace. In a marriage, they imagined, their husband would earn the money and pay the bills, maintain the car, and fix things when they broke. What they didn't imagine, however, was that the job of homemaker and full-time mother is perhaps one of the most challenging jobs for a woman with ADD.

Escape into the Workplace

Ironically, some of those women who opted for becoming homemakers later decided that life at work was easier to manage. One woman worked 30 hours a week in a job she enjoyed. After her son and then, shortly thereafter, her daughter were diagnosed with ADD, she decided to stay home full-time to provide her children with the structure and support she felt they needed. Several months after quitting her job, she sought an ADD evaluation for herself.

She tearfully recounted that she had never felt more disorganized and less functional in her life. Since she was home full-time, she felt she should do the housecleaning herself. Without the structure that her workday had imposed, she found that she was completely scattered. Laundry went unfinished as she hurried out the door to volunteer at school. Housework was done sporadically. Her husband came home each night to a harried, tired wife, and to a messy house. Normally a patient man, he finally asked "*What* have you been doing all day?"

Before, when she had been working, she had been able to hire someone to do the housework on a weekly basis. She had a quiet, orderly workplace in which to spend six hours a day and was able to devote her afternoons to carpooling and children's activities. After her ADD diagnosis, she realized that the competing tasks, frequent interruptions, and lack of structure at home were too much for her. She finally returned, with relief, to her quiet part-time job.

HOMEMAKING AND ADD

Diary of an ADD Housewife

Charlene is the mother of two children. She has been diagnosed with the hyperactive-impulsive type of ADD, as has one of her sons. For all of those women with ADD who quietly, maybe shamefully, wonder, "Am I the only one who's like this?," Charlene agreed to describe a "day in the life."

> Oh, God. You mean you want me to write down everything I do for an entire day? I don't know if I can. I'll either spend the whole day at the kitchen table trying to figure out what to write, or I'll get busy and forget to write anything. (We agreed that she could just recount the events of the preceding day orally—to rescue her from this very much ADD dilemma!)
>
> Well, let's see…I'm embarrassed to tell you some things. I'm afraid of what you'll think. Oh well, like sometimes I don't get dressed all day, unless I have to go somewhere. And when I do have to go somewhere, it takes me forever to get ready. But sometimes I just throw on my coat over my nightgown if I have to drive one of the kids to school. One of them is always late.
>
> OK. So what do I do in the morning? I don't really have a routine. I guess I just get up. Getting up is really hard. I'm always tired, because I love to stay up late and read or watch TV when it's quiet—so I'm always tired. I keep calling to the kids to get up and get ready for school, but sometimes I'm not there making sure they're doing it. Things are

always crazy at my house. The kids lose things. I lose things. I get so frustrated with them in the morning that sometimes I start yelling.

My day doesn't have any plan. I just go through it. I know a few things, like if my son has a dentist appointment or something, but other than that it's just crazy. It's impossible for me to keep on track. I'll go upstairs to get dressed, get a phone call, talk on the phone for a while, and then start doing something upstairs without ever getting dressed. It's so hard for me to get organized.

When I try really hard at one thing, then everything else goes to pot. Like I'll get all involved in redecorating one room, but then I get behind on the laundry and don't feel like cooking dinner. We don't have any routines for the kids or for me. Half the time I try to do two or three things at once. My husband says he's never seen anyone who could be so busy and get so little accomplished.

The "Job" of Homemaker from an ADD Perspective

Why does Charlene, like so many other homemakers with ADD, have such a difficult time? Let's take a look at the characteristics of an ideal workplace environment and compare them to the conditions in which a homemaker works:

Ideal ADD Workplace Conditions	*Homemaker's Workplace Conditions*
Quiet, nondistracting workplace	Frequently noisy and distracting
Guidance in priority setting	No guidance in priority setting available
Assistance in maintaining priorities as workplace demands shift	No assistance available in maintaining priorities
Clear guidelines about duties and responsibilities	No clear guidelines; must develop job description oneself
Friendly environment in which efforts are noted and appreciated	Little positive feedback given for efforts
Periods of uninterrupted time in which to accomplish tasks requiring concentration	Frequent interruptions; very difficult to arrange uninterrupted blocks of time

Ideal ADD Workplace *Conditions* (continued)	*Homemaker's Workplace* *Conditions* (continued)
Work assignments are stimulating and interesting	Work assignments are boring and repetitive
Minimize or eliminate demands to oversee or monitor work of others	Large portion of job involves supervision and monitoring of others
Minimize pressures, such as overtime work, to avoid burnout	Overtime requirements are frequent, unpredictable, non-negotiable
Ability to control and limit the flow of competing work demands	Need to be always responsive to workplace demands, with little opportunity to control work flow

If we consider the job of homemaker-mother from an ADD perspective, we notice that it involves many conditions resulting in maximum stress for minimum reward. Women with ADD—whose homes may be in a shambles, whose laundry is rarely done, whose meals are haphazard, last-minute affairs, and whose children (who are likely to have ADD as well) frequently misbehave—are prone to blame themselves: "Why do I do such a poor job of something that anyone should be able to accomplish?" If we compare the workplace conditions of a homemaker to desirable workplace conditions for an adult with ADD, we quickly see that they are almost directly opposite. Not only does society expect women to have primary responsibility for maintaining the home and preparing meals, but it also expects them to be the primary parent and the "emotional command center" of the home. Mothers are expected to be patient, understanding, encouraging, supportive, and much more focused on the needs of their family than on their own needs.

A mother who feels "driven crazy" by the frequent interruptions of her children, who needs to take time away from her children to ease her frayed nerves, who becomes irritated, impatient, or angry, may see herself, and be seen by everyone around her, as a "bad mother." When the forces of ADD and PMS combine relentlessly every month, these women are likely to feel an even greater loss of control. Women with ADD need to understand themselves, and be understood by their husbands, their families, and friends. These "bad mothers" whose children misbehave more frequently, and who may raise their voices and lose their tempers more often than they would like, need to be understood as women with ADD who are struggling valiantly with demands that are sometimes difficult, if not impossible, to meet.

LIFE-MANAGEMENT SKILLS

What Can Women with ADD Do to Manage Their Lives Better?

Give yourself a break! Often the biggest struggle is an internal one. Societal expectations have been deeply ingrained in many women. Even if a loving husband said, "Don't worry about it," women would place demands on themselves. Breaking out of a mold that doesn't fit can take time and effort. Psychotherapy with a therapist who really understands your struggles with ADD may help you to shed your impossible expectations of yourself.

Educate your husband about ADD and how it affects you. Your husband may feel anger and resentment toward an ill-kept house or ill-behaved children, assuming that you "just don't care." He needs to appreciate the full brunt of ADD's impact on you. Get him on your side so that both of you can plan ways to make your life at home more accommodating and ADD-friendly.

It's only spilled milk! Try to create an "ADD-friendly" environment in your home. If you can approach your ADD, and that of your children, with acceptance and good humor, explosions will decrease and you'll save more energy for the positive side of things.

Simplify your life. You are probably overbooked, and chances are, your children are too. Look for ways to reduce commitments so that you're not always pressed and hurried.

Don't hang around "super homemakers" who can't understand your problems. So many women describe friends or neighbors who make them feel terrible by comparison: Their houses are immaculate and their children are always clean, neat, and well behaved. Don't put yourself in situations that can lead to impossible expectations and negative comparisons.

Build a support group for yourself. One woman with ADD related that housework was such drudgery that she often couldn't bring herself to do it. One of her techniques, however, was to invite a friend, who shared similar tendencies, to keep her company while she completed some particularly odious task. A women's ADD support group reported that they formed housework teams. Three or four women with ADD went as a group to each of their homes to do housework. This allowed the work to be done more quickly and provided mutual support and socializing at the same time.

Build in "time-outs" daily. Time-outs are essential when you have ADD and are raising children. It's easy to not find time for them, though, because they require planning. Make them routine so that you don't have to keep planning and juggling. For example, ask your husband to commit to two blocks of time on the weekend when he will take the kids away from the house. Arrange for a regular babysitter several times a week.

Don't place yourself in burnout. One ADD mother of two ADD children, who was doing a great job of parenting her children, was also able to recognize her limitations. With two such challenging children, she arranged for sleep-away camp for a month each summer. She also arranged for separate, brief visits to grandparents. This allowed her to spend time with each child without his having to compete with his brother.

Eliminate and delegate. Look at tasks that you require of yourself at home. Can some of these chores be eliminated? Can you find a way to hire a person to do some of them?

Learn child behavior management techniques. On the outside looking in, it may be easy for other parents to judge you if your children misbehave. What any parent of an ADD child knows is that he or she doesn't respond to the usual admonishments and limits the way non-ADD kids do. You've got a super-challenging job. Get the best training you can find. There are numerous excellent books dealing with behavior-management techniques for children with ADD. Some of these books are listed in the Resource List.

Look for positive experiences to share with your kids. As an ADD mother of ADD children, it can be very easy to slip into a pattern of admonishing them for misbehavior and later ignoring them because you feel tired and overwhelmed by the demands of parenting. Both you and your children will feel and function better if you take time out to have fun. Look for activities in which you can enjoy your kids without needing to correct them frequently so that you can all relax and enjoy each other's company. Active outdoor activities can be good. A "quiet time" with your child before bedtime is another potentially positive activity. Talk together or read a story for a few minutes.

Get help for PMS or menopausal symptoms. They are likely to be more severe than in other women. Managing the destabilizing effect of your hormonal fluctuations is a critical part of managing your ADD.

Focus more on the things you love. Don't just measure your success in terms of made beds and washed dishes. Learn to appreciate yourself, and look for people to share your time with who appreciate you, too!

In summary, as a woman with ADD, you face special challenges that are often not understood and appreciated. Monthly hormonal fluctuations tend to worsen ADD symptoms, which are already difficult. While men with ADD are often able to find caretakers to provide a support system—wives, secretaries, subordinates—women with ADD continue to feel strong societal pressure to provide those caretaker functions for others.

If you are a woman with ADD, the most positive thing you can do for yourself is to understand and learn to accept yourself. Don't join the rest of society in condemning your housekeeping or parenting style. Build support and understanding through educating your family about ADD, through psychotherapy to build self-esteem and coping strategies, and through seeking the support of other women like yourself. Celebrate your spontaneity, your creativity, and your caring nature. And remember—don't sweat the small stuff!

11

Self-Advocacy for Adults with ADD: Evaluating and Creating Resources

Self-Advocacy for Adults with ADD: Evaluating and Creating Resources

A DD adults have been self-advocates from the start. First, adults who were parents of children with ADD joined ADD organizations to fight for the needs of their children. Then, as many of these adults recognized ADD traits in themselves, it was only a matter of time until these activist parents also became self-advocates. Self-help groups for adults with ADD have sprung up across the United States during the past several years, many operating independently of any larger group affiliation. CH.A.D.D. (Children and Adults with Attention Deficit Disorder), whose original charter was framed to advocate for the needs of children, initially resisted pressure from the adult ADD sector. ADD adults, who are undeniably insistent, eventually made themselves heard by the CH.A.D.D. hierarchy. CH.A.D.D. formed an Adult Issues Committee; and in 1994 CH.A.D.D. changed its name to include the word "adults" in its title. This is yet another example of adults with ADD advocating vigorously and successfully for themselves. ADDA (Attention Deficit Disorder Association), another large national organization focusing on ADD issues, has been very active in promoting the needs of adults with ADD. In 1995, ADDA organized its first national adult ADD conference.

In the spirit of encouraging self-advocacy for adults with ADD, this chapter focuses on resources: how to evaluate those that already exist and how you can help to create resources in your community.

Buyer Beware! Common Misconceptions About Adult ADD in the Professional Community

Because adult ADD is such a new field, there is a tremendous need for training professionals to diagnose and treat adult ADD. Some professionals who present themselves as "experts" on adult ADD may actually have little information or may even be misinformed. Few professionals have extensive experience and/or training in working with ADD adults. It is essential to educate yourself in order to judge whether you are receiving appropriate treatment.

Here are some unfortunate experiences that ADD adults have had when seeking treatment. The majority of professionals described in the following vignettes were qualified to practice their professions and enjoyed good reputations in their communities. Unfortunately, they were operating with inadequate knowledge, and sometimes incorrect information, in their efforts to treat an adult with ADD.

"You can't possibly have ADD if you have been able to complete a Ph.D."

This statement was made to a highly intelligent, but struggling scientist who sought diagnosis and treatment from a psychiatrist whose experience was primarily with ADD children. This psychiatrist's statement was probably based on the fact that many children with ADD experience school difficulties. He was apparently not familiar, however, with that subset of people with ADD who are highly gifted. In fact, high intelligence and Attention Deficit Disorder are not an uncommon combination. Dr. Ned Hallowell, for example, is a noted psychiatrist, an expert on ADD, and an ADD adult himself.

"It's very unlikely that you have ADD, since you have been able to gain admission into this competitive university without prior diagnosis and treatment."

This is just another variant on the above theme. The university-affiliated psychiatrist who made this statement diagnosed the young woman in question with bipolar disorder, misinterpreting her hyperactivity as a hypomanic state. Fortunately, she was able to find another physician in her college community who was expert in ADD and who could correctly identify and treat it.

"Even if you do have ADD, what does that have to do with our couple's counseling work?"

This question was asked by a psychologist working with a couple in marital counseling. The husband had just been diagnosed with ADD and wanted to work on ADD issues as part of his couples therapy. This psychologist apparently was not very familiar with the profound impact of ADD on relationships due to problems with intimacy, poor listening skills, poor communication patterns, impulsivity, and a general tendency to create a level of chaos and confusion in a household.

"Well, I don't know much about it, but if your psychologist thinks you have ADD, I'll be willing to write you a prescription for Ritalin."

The well-intentioned general practitioner who made this statement did not do his patient a favor. He was not trained to provide guidance and supervision about dosage levels and frequency, nor did he seem to realize that other medications, or combinations of medications, might be more helpful. Other adults with ADD have brought similar tales to their ADD support groups. The use of medication in treating ADD is much more complex than the prescription of some standard dose of stimulants; and it requires close supervision, especially in the early stages, as dosage levels are adjusted, and combinations of medication are considered.

"It doesn't really matter whether you're depressed or whether you have ADD. The treatment is basically the same—medication and psychotherapy."

This statement was made by a neurologist to a patient who was trying to sort out the issues she was struggling with. As many adults with ADD—misdiagnosed as depressed—can attest, standard treatment for depression, that is, antidepressant medication and insight-oriented psychotherapy, may help treat depression but does nothing for ADD symptoms. In such contexts, ADD symptoms are often interpreted psychologically rather than understood as symptoms of a neurochemical disorder. This kind of misinterpretation can do great damage to an individual's self-esteem and sense of efficacy.

"The best way to diagnose ADD is to give you stimulant medication and then to measure your response to it."

This statement contains two errors. First, a positive response to stimulant medication does not confirm an ADD diagnosis. Most people experience better focus and more alertness on a stimulant medication, similar to how most people respond to the caffeine in a cup of coffee. Second, there is no instrument that is accepted in ADD research as a definitive measure of ADD. Although a number of computerized tests have been developed, they are appropriately used only as part of an assessment battery.

Given all these statements from educated professionals that misinformed or did a disservice to an adult with ADD, how can you be sure you're seeing a professional who will guide you in the right direction? Refer back to Chapter 2, which provides you with a list of questions to ask professionals in order to better understand their training and experience in treating adults with ADD.

EDUCATE YOURSELF ABOUT ADULT ADD

If self-education is the name of the game, how do you go about doing this? Fortunately, this task is much easier now than it would have been only three or four years ago. A number of organizations across the country are devoted to adult ADD issues. These organizations and conferences are listed in the Resource List. They hold annual conferences that offer a wide array of talks on topics pertaining to adult ADD. However, most of these seem to be clustered primarily in the Midwest and on the East Coast; there is a strong need for more *regional* adult ADD conferences.

Most people assume that their physician or therapist is completely informed and up-to-date on whatever malady concerns them. Although one hopes that this is usually the case, when you are seeking treatment for adult ADD from someone who is not yet expert in the field, it may be best to approach your treatment as an active partnership in which you are both seeking to learn the best treatment options.

It is also important to keep in mind that no single professional, even if he or she is highly knowledgeable about adult ADD, can provide all of the services you may need. Because ADD affects all aspects of your life, you may need to consult career counselors, marital counselors, financial managers, tutors, and organizational trainers, among others, as you work to improve different aspects of your life.

Financial Support

Limited Funds, Lack of Insurance Coverage

Unfortunately the options are limited at the moment, whether or not your funds are limited. Here are a few possibilities that you can try:

Apply for services through the Department of Rehabilitative Services (DRS). The DRS has offices in each state, with branch offices in most major communities. Its charter is to serve the needs of people whose disabilities lead them to be unemployed or underemployed. It can provide and/or fund a range of services including diagnostic testing, career planning, and assistance in finding a more appropriate job. DRS has, on occasion, even helped to fund educational expenses in adults with ADD or LD. Realistically, though, the range and level of services often provided through DRS are limited, and the evaluations that are sometimes received through DRS may not be as thorough or accurate as you would hope. This is true largely because DRS cannot pay an adequate fee to those who provide evaluations, which often leads to evaluations that are rather cursory and sometimes inaccurate. Again, buyer beware! Others though, have had excellent experiences when seeking services through DRS. All of their services are free of charge to the client.

Seek services through your local community college. Any student who is enrolled in courses at a community college and who has a documented disability is eligible for disability services offered on campus. These services vary from college to college, but many schools have excellent programs that teach organization, time management, study skills, and provide tutoring for specific academic subjects.

Ask your therapist or physician for a reduced fee if you are unemployed, uninsured, or marginally employed. Many therapists are willing to reduce their fees, either on a permanent or temporary basis, until their clients have a job and insurance coverage. It never hurts to ask!

Attend Adult ADD Support Groups. Many support groups have sprung up in communities across the country. These are not intended to be a substitute for psychotherapy; but they can provide excellent sources of information, networking about resources in the community, as well as an opportunity to get the support of fellow ADD sufferers.

How Can I Find an Adult ADD Group?

Adult ADD groups have been mentioned as one source of a no-cost or low-cost service for adults with ADD. Because such groups have a great potential to educate, provide resources, and provide support, they deserve to be discussed at greater length. You can obtain information about adult groups by contacting your nearest CH.A.D.D. or ADDA group. (See the Resource List.)

There are many adult groups already in existence, and more are starting up every day. If no adult support group exists in your community, you should consider becoming one of the founders of a group. Don't despair. All of the other groups have been started by adults with ADD just like yourself.

There are several different models of Adult ADD groups. One model has developed as an offshoot of CH.A.D.D. parent-support groups. This model has a more formalized structure that includes a steering committee and a structured, information-oriented program. Such groups typically invite experts on adult ADD from the community to give presentations. At other times they may organize structured discussion groups among themselves. They may develop resource lists of professionals in the community, as well as a lending library of books on ADD that members may borrow. This type of group offers many benefits, especially in imparting accurate information about diagnosis and treatment issues. Large groups tend to lend themselves to this more structured model.

Another group model is that of the small, informal support group in which there is no agenda other than to provide mutual support and an opportunity to share and interact with other adults with ADD. Such groups may choose to meet more often than the large, information-oriented groups. Some support groups offer both models—a monthly informational session as well as smaller, more informal groups. The smaller groups may meet after the large session or may even meet at a different time and place.

An adult ADD group can start small and can grow, as more people join and become committed to its growth. Don't feel that you can't take on the formation of a group because you have ADD. Just keep your goals limited, and look for two or three others to work with you in forming the group.

Spreading the Word

What Can I Do to Help Educate Professionals in My Community About Adult ADD?

If you are an adult already diagnosed with ADD, you are already aware of the shortage of professionals who are educated and experienced about adult ADD. Even in metropolitan areas where there are likely to be more trained professionals, the competition for a place in their busy schedules can be fierce.

At this time there is tremendous need to develop educational training seminars about ADD for professionals. If there is a CH.A.D.D. or ADDA organization in your community, it may be a good idea to join that organization and to suggest that CH.A.D.D. or ADDA sponsor, or at least initiate, a professional training seminar in your area. The national headquarters of both CH.A.D.D. and ADDA can provide the local organization with lists of recognized adult ADD experts who may be interested in providing such training.

In other words, don't just sit there. Do something! ADD adults have been amazingly effective in gaining recognition and understanding of their disorder in a short period of time. Your best means of finding the assistance you need is to join the ADD adult activist bandwagon in your community. The national offices of CH.A.D.D. and ADDA will assuredly be supportive as you undertake local efforts to develop adult ADD resources.

12

Success Stories: From College Years to Senior Years

Success Stories: From College Years to Senior Years

The following stories are shared to offer you many reasons for optimism as you begin your journey toward learning about ADD, how it affects you, and how to build a positive future by learning to manage your ADD. All of the following stories are true, although names and details have been changed to protect the privacy of people involved. Each of them is happy to share his or her story with the reader in the hope that it will inspire you to make the life changes that will benefit you. The youngest person described is 19; the oldest is 74. As you will see when you read their stories, in spite of their ADD, they are all unique individuals, with different needs, who found a wide range of approaches and solutions to their problems.

SUCCESS WITH ADD IN THE COLLEGE YEARS

Erin

Erin is a spunky, strong-willed, and sometimes argumentative young woman. Her teenage years were full of battles—with her mother, who was overly attached; and with her father, with whom she engaged in frequent power struggles. School had always been difficult for her, and she found that studying, amid the noise and confusion of family life, was completely impossible. She had not developed any consistent study habits or study skills. Outside of the house, Erin felt little self-confidence. Her social world revolved around her part-time job.

When Erin sought an ADD evaluation, she had been struggling through a community college for three years, earning mediocre grades, dropping courses each term, and feeling little sense of direction. She had recently transferred to a four-year state college close to her home, but fared no better in her first semester there. A college counselor suggested that she seek an evaluation for Attention Deficit Disorder.

The neuropsychologist who evaluated Erin was more familiar with test patterns in children with AD/HD. Because the signs of her ADD were more subtle, she did not receive an ADD diagnosis. Erin, however, was a persistent young woman. With the encouragement of her counselor, she sought another psychologist, who recognized and diagnosed her ADD. Unfortunately, Erin's experience with misdiagnosis is fairly common among college students who are not diagnosed until their college years; they are likely to show more subtle signs of ADD and have developed many compensatory techniques that may mask ADD.

Unlike some college students who are brought for treatment by worried parents, Erin sought treatment on her own and showed tremendous motivation from the start. Her treatment involved medication, psychotherapy, very active participation in an adult support group, and educational support as well. This multimodal approach worked very well for Erin. She was clearly determined to take charge of her life and find a direction for herself.

Throughout her treatment Erin focused on many different issues, including her discomfort with dating, her dissatisfaction with her weight, her conflictual relationship with both parents, and her insecurity in social situations. Over a period of time she was very successful in losing weight, felt much more socially confident, and had begun to develop an adult–adult relationship with her parents. She also worked on her lifelong feelings of "being different," which many individuals with ADD share. As she learned to temper her ADD tendencies toward being a bit blunt, argumentative, and outspoken, her relationships at home and with her friends improved.

Erin approached her ADD academic issues both in therapy and through the Student Disability Services office on her college campus. Through her counseling, she chose a more appropriate career path and worked on planning and organization skills. At school she learned to advocate for her needs with her professors, and she developed a very close, cooperative relationship with her academic adviser. Medication enhanced her ability to focus and concentrate. All of these factors worked together to improve her grades.

As Erin terminated her counseling sessions she was seriously dating someone for the first time, had moved out of her parents' house, was earning good grades (although she continued to struggle a bit with attention problems), and had become a campus leader on ADD/LD issues. Her confidence was high, and she had learned to see her ADD as a fact of life she was learning to manage, not as a disability that prevented success.

Matt

Matt was a college student who entered treatment for ADD under very different circumstances from Erin. He had been diagnosed with ADD in childhood and had intermittently taken Ritalin throughout his elementary and high school years. His intelligence was in the gifted range; however, his high school grades had been mediocre. He began his freshman year in college, away from home, at a school more known for its social life than its academic life. Although his parents had been skeptical about his choice of college, they had allowed him to make it independently.

Matt was brought for consultation by his mother after nearly failing his freshman year of college. He had not taken medication and had sought no support services on campus during freshman year, serenely believing that, with his intelligence, he would waltz his way through school. After many adventures, one broken heart, and very little studying, a very chastened Matt sat in the psychologist's office with his mother.

Counseling during that summer left Matt convinced of several things: he needed to resume taking stimulant medication; he needed more structure in his life; and he would be more likely to succeed in college by living at home and attending a local university.

During the following school year, Matt's counseling focused on many issues. One of the major tasks before him was to learn to manage his time better. Matt is a very attractive, intelligent, highly verbal, and intense young man. When he had been away at school, he had been drawn into several fascinating friendships, spending many nights in conversation and debate. He gradually learned to temper this tendency to become immersed in relationships and made time to study each day. Matt learned to use a day planner to plan long-term assignments and developed the habit of setting daily goals for himself. One of the creative ways Matt learned to satisfy his extrovert needs while studying was by forming study groups before major exams. Matt's grades improved during his first semester at home, and he was on the honor roll by his second semester.

When Matt's grades were no longer a primary focus of concern, his counseling shifted toward longer-term planning: the choice of a major that would lead toward a career for which he would be suited and the decision whether to remain at home or transfer to another school.

Ultimately, because Matt had become so successful with the supports offered by his physician, his therapist, and his tutor, he elected to remain at home. Matt continued to earn excellent grades and graduated with honors three years later, much better prepared for adventures in the wider world.

Although both Matt and Erin benefited from multiple supports, the changes each of them needed took them in almost opposite directions. Matt needed the ongoing structure and support provided by living with his parents. He was able to realize this only after an initial failure in attending college away from home. Although Matt tried to deny his ADD, Erin—who was not diagnosed until young adulthood—faced her ADD head on. Her path to success led her away from home and parents and toward more confidence and independence.

ADD IN MIDLIFE

Elaine

Elaine's treatment for ADD symptoms was not her first foray into therapy. She had been in psychotherapy for several years following her divorce, struggling to cope with anxiety, depression, and feelings of inadequacy. In particular, she was troubled by her relationship with "Hank," a man she had met following her divorce. Although her relationship with Hank was far from perfect, she had little self-confidence after being left by her husband of many years. She believed that she could choose only between Hank and a lonely life alone.

She sought an ADD evaluation after reading several articles about adult ADD. Elaine's daughter, now in her twenties, had academic troubles throughout her school years and showed many symptoms of ADD. As Elaine learned more about ADD, she began to strongly suspect that both she and her young adult daughter needed treatment. After her ADD evaluation she started on a regimen of medication (both antidepressant and stimulant) and ultimately decided to switch from more traditional psychotherapy to work with a therapist who specialized in treating ADD adults.

When Elaine began her ADD treatment she held a low-paying part-time job, and she was very dependent on alimony payments from her ex-husband. She felt enormous anxiety about her future but had no sense of which career direction to pursue. Elaine had worked on and off throughout her marriage, but always in low-paying low-level positions. Despite her college degree, she had little self-confidence and had never held a professional-level job.

A career history was taken, and it soon became obvious that many of the jobs Elaine had taken were very ill-suited to an adult with ADD. She had struggled with, but ultimately failed in, jobs that were detail oriented and that primarily involved paperwork. She enjoyed contact with students and recalled that, years before, she had also enjoyed a job that involved providing social services. Currently Elaine was working as a part-time health aid in a school and was struggling with night courses in nursing. Her plan was eventually to earn a nursing degree.

Because she had struggled in college and was continuing to struggle academically in her nursing courses, a learning-disability evaluation was recommended. Her LD evaluation revealed difficulties with memory, organization, and especially with written expression. All of this information was essential as Elaine continued to work with her therapist in charting a career course. Elaine's therapist helped her to examine her choice of a nursing career. Given her difficulty with memory, with organization, and with handling details, it appeared that nursing was probably not the most compatible choice. She began to explore the possibility of earning a master's degree in social work. She felt that would satisfy her desire to work with people and would call on her interpersonal strengths but would not tax her areas of academic weakness to the same degree as a nursing career. Elaine began to explore social-work programs.

In order to gain support and develop her writing skills, Elaine began taking night classes in writing for learning-disabled adults and also hired a writing tutor recommended by her therapist. She began working on her writing skills months before she was to enter a social-work master's degree program. In fact, she even used a tutor to assist her in writing her application essays and in completing her application forms (both tasks that are often very difficult for individuals with ADD).

With growing confidence, Elaine applied and was selected for a full-time job. The new job, unfortunately, required detailed paperwork. Elaine and her therapist worked together to develop organizational systems to keep her paperwork in order. They also focused on ways to disclose her ADD at work, when appropriate, and ways to deal with a rather critical and unsupportive supervisor. Elaine continued to grow in her knowledge of herself, her ADD, and how to manage ADD symptoms on the job.

Several months later she was accepted into a master's degree program and again, she worked with her therapist in developing academic survival skills. She obtained a course syllabus early, bought all the books, and began reading them during the summer before she began classes. She continued to work intensively with her writing tutor, who helped her organize and then edit her first graduate-school paper. To Elaine's delight she earned an A on her first paper—a triumph in view of her learning disability in written language.

Two years after beginning treatment for her ADD, Elaine finds herself in a very different situation—working full-time, advocating effectively for herself at work, attending graduate school on a very appropriate career track, earning A's in her courses, and generally feeling hopeful and empowered. She is learning to recognize the limits imposed by her ADD and is becoming much better at setting limits with others. Life isn't perfect. She still becomes disorganized at times and feels overwhelmed at exam time. But, generally, Elaine has learned to appreciate herself, and to manage her ADD; and she is hard at work building a life and a future that will suit her much better than did her past choices.

Dan

Dan is a very bright man in the computer field who sought treatment for anxiety, depression, and ADD. Dan found himself in the wrong job, with the wrong supervisor, and had reached a point of chronic anger, anxiety, and rock-bottom self-confidence over the course of several years. His energy, intelligence, and creativity had propelled him to high levels in the computer field; unfortunately, as sometimes happens, he was promoted to a job that was all wrong for him, a job involving primary responsibility for multiple, simultaneous long-term projects.

Dan's distractibility and organizational problems led him to frequently lose focus on his tasks. As his frustrations increased, so did his interpersonal difficulties. He was impatient, lost his temper, and began having difficulty working with other people. Dan described himself as having "rough edges": "Sometimes I jump over steps and do things faster than other people. I need to learn to listen more."

Unfortunately there was a terrible personality mismatch between Dan and his supervisor. When he asked for accommodations, they were given in a demeaning, almost punitive fashion. For example, when Dan asked for more structure in his job, his supervisor made a unilateral decision to take several projects away from him. He micro-managed Dan in a very critical fashion as he attempted to complete the one project that continued to be assigned to him. Dan's anxiety and chronic depression led him to become increasingly more dysfunctional. Finally he reached the point where he felt he was simply "walking through his days," accomplishing almost nothing.

Treatment for Dan's ADD focused simultaneously on his emotional outbursts, his intense anxiety attacks, his chronic depression, and his distractibility and disorganization. He was placed on a combination of medications. In therapy, Dan began to learn about himself, understanding his ADD and how it affected him. Dan also learned to get back in touch with his strengths. His areas of dysfunction and vulnerability had been so much in the forefront that he had lost sight of his strengths. As his depression lifted somewhat, Dan began to network outside of his company. This networking put him in touch with people who had known him earlier, and who respected and appreciated his considerable abilities. He soon began to learn of other job possibilities.

Dan approached job hunting in a very "ADD-wise" fashion. He realized that he was at his best when he was doing creative problem solving—finding immediate solutions to immediate problems. In his previous position he was expected to manage several long-term projects simultaneously. Instead of being able to use his creativity, his job required him to manage and track multiple detailed projects. In looking for a new job, he looked for a more informal, flexible environment—one in which his expertise and creativity would be used and which minimized managerial responsibilities.

Within several months Dan found such a job; although greatly relieved to be leaving the years of personal torment behind him, Dan entered the new job with some fear and trepidation. What do I do now if I feel disorganized or overwhelmed? How do I communicate about my ADD? Do I disclose my ADD? Fortunately, Dan had chosen well. In his new job he felt supported and appreciated. He had been hired as a troubleshooter and problem solver—tasks for which he was well suited.

The focus now shifted to learning to manage his ADD. Dan learned to use a day planner religiously. He learned to set limits on his natural enthusiasm and helpfulness, which had tended to create chronic overload. Dan worked to manage his distractibility, learning to shut his office door during periods of the day. He also learned to manage his hyper-focusing tendency, which had caused him to miss meetings and commitments in the past. Dan still developed periodic anxiety in his new job when he found himself in overload; however, these periods decreased in frequency and intensity as he continued to learn how to manage his ADD patterns.

After more than a year in his new job and more than two years of treatment for ADD, Dan felt calmer, more positive, and more confident than ever. Like a lion tamer, Dan learned to harness and direct the energy and creativity that are part of his ADD but rests ever-mindful of the potentially destructive force of old patterns. When ADD rears its head from time to time, he knows how to maneuver the lion back into his cage.

It's Never Too Late...

Alice

Alice is a 74-year-old retired school teacher who sought an ADD evaluation after reading a checklist of adult ADD symptoms. She told her story with humor, reflecting the determination, ingenuity, and creativity with which she had lived her 74 years.

She grew up as the second of three children in an academic family. Her father was on the faculty of one of the top women's colleges. Although quiet and painfully shy, she recalls several creative adventures that went largely unappreciated by parents who wanted a more docile, well-behaved little girl. Once, as a four-year-old, she was inspired to make a crayon drawing on the wall, which she proudly displayed to her mother. Expecting praise, the tiny budding artist was crushed when her mother punished her for scribbling on the wall. Another time, at Sunday school, Alice wandered out of her classroom. Eventually finding another child to play with, she had great fun crawling on the floor, making noises, pretending to be an animal. Alice was blissfully unaware that she had ruined her pretty organdy dress until her dismayed father finally found her playing under a table.

A few years later, Alice recalled, her hometown was flooded. She became so fascinated by the flood waters, throwing pebbles and swishing sticks in the water, that she completely lost track of time. Arriving home very late, she learned that her distraught mother had called the police! All of these stories depict a very active and curious little girl, engrossed in her own activities, oblivious to the passage of time and often oblivious to the reactions she provoked in others.

In school, Alice recalls feeling lost much of the time; her curious, wandering mind often strayed from the topic of the teacher's lecture, to her great embarrassment when she was called on. Despite this distractibility, through the strength of her intelligence, she went on to earn a college degree.

Alice married, divorced at a time when divorce was much less common, and raised two children alone, working as an art teacher. During these years teaching art, her ADD was actually an asset in many ways. She developed countless fun, creative projects for her students and always had a soft spot in her heart for students who struggled as she had.

So why, you might ask, did this spunky, creative woman, who had raised two children and been a much-loved art teacher, seek treatment for ADD at age 74? As often happens with ADD adults, she functioned better when her life was structured, by the needs of children and the demands of her job. As a retiree she found herself feeling depressed, isolated, and completely disorganized. She had lots of ideas, but no initiative to carry them out. Her small apartment had become totally cluttered, and even small daily tasks felt overwhelming at times. By chance she read an article reviewing a book on ADD in adults. In reading the symptom checklist noted in the article, she suddenly recognized herself. "So that's what I've been struggling with all these years!"

Fortunately, Alice was able to find a physician who took her concerns about ADD seriously and was willing to prescribe both antidepressant and stimulant medication for her. Six months later, her life was back on track. The guidance she received during counseling, in combination with medication, allowed her to follow through on goals and helped her in different aspects of her life. She enrolled in art courses, become active in a local church, and began to develop several very interesting friendships. At home she was much more organized and went about her day in a reasonably efficient fashion, leaving plenty of time for fun. And, true to her spunky self, she was happy to have her story told here, to benefit other seniors who may wonder if they, too, have ADD.

CONCLUSION

From the teen years to the senior years, all of these people were able to move from a feeling that their lives were out of control to a sense of purpose, direction, and growing self-confidence. Like the people portrayed in this chapter, you also can take charge of your ADD. Learn as much as you can about ADD in adults. Be active in your search for good, effective treatment. Form or join a support group. Try to surround yourself with positive, encouraging people. Don't just focus on what you can't do. Learn to recognize your special gifts and abilities, and look for a way to use them. There are many successful people who happen to have ADD. This book can help you to count yourself among them.

Resource List

The following list is not exhaustive, but it is a good starting point for accessing the growing fund of information on adult ADD. References to other resource lists are included.

Books

ADD Adults

A Comprehensive Guide to Attention Deficit Disorder in Adults: Research, Diagnosis, and Treatment. Edited by Kathleen G. Nadeau, Ph.D. New York: Brunner/Mazel, 1995.

Answers to Distraction. By Edward M. Hallowell, M.D., and John Ratey, M.D. New York: Pantheon Books, 1995.

Attention Deficit Disorder and the Law: A Guide for Advocates. By Peter S. Latham, J.D., and Patricia H. Latham, J.D., 1992. (Available through JKL Communications, P.O. Box 40157, Washington, D.C. 20016.)

Attention Deficit Disorder: Practical Help for Sufferers and Their Spouses. By Lynn Weiss, Ph.D. Houston, TX: Taylor, 1992.

The Hyperactive Child, Adolescent, and Adult: Attention Deficit Disorder Through the Lifespan. By Paul Wender, M.D. New York: Oxford University Press, 1987.

Succeeding in the Workplace—Attention Deficit Disorder and Learning Disabilities in the Workplace: A Guide for Success. By Peter S. Latham, J.D., and Patricia H. Latham, J.D., 1994. (Available through JKL Communications, P.O. Box 40157, Washington, D.C. 20016.)

Women with Attention Deficit Disorder: Embracing Disorganization at Home and in the Workplace. By Sari Solden, M.S. Grass Valley, CA: Underwood Books, 1995.

You Mean I'm Not Lazy, Stupid, or Crazy?!: A Self-Help Book for Adults with Attention Deficit Disorder. By Kate Kelly, and Peggy Ramundo. New York: Scribner's, 1995.

ADD and Higher Education

ADD and the College Student: A Guide for High School and College Students with Attention Deficit Disorder. Edited by Patricia O. Quinn, M.D. New York: Magination Press, 1994.

The K & W Guide for the Learning Disabled: A Resource Book for Students, Parents and Professionals. By Marybeth Kravets, M.A., and Imy F. Wax, M.S., New York: HarperCollins, 1992.

Peterson's Guide to Colleges with Programs for Students with Learning Disabilities. Edited by Charles T. Mangrum, III, and Stephen S. Strichart. Princeton, NJ: Peterson's Guides, 1992.

Survival Guide for College Students with ADD or LD. By Kathleen G. Nadeau, Ph.D. New York: Magination Press, 1994.

Unlocking Potential: College and Other Choices for Learning Disabled People— A Step-by-Step Guide. By Barbara Scheiber, and Jeanne Talpers. Chevy Chase, MD: Adler & Adler, 1987.

Parenting ADD Children and Adolescents

Hyperkinetic Children: A Neuropsychological Approach. By C. Keith Connors. Thousand Oaks, CA: Sage, 1986.

Negotiating the Parent/Adolescent Conflict. By Arthur L. Robin and Sharon L. Foster. New York: Guilford Press, 1990.

Attention Deficit/Hyperactivity Disorder. By Russell A. Barkley. New York: Guilford Press, 1990.

Defiant Children. By Russell A. Barkley. New York: Guilford Press, 1987.

Driven to Distraction: Recognizing and Coping with Attention Deficit Disorder from Childhood Through Adulthood. By Edward M. Hallowell, M.D. and John Ratey, M.D. New York: Pantheon Books, 1994.

ADULT ADD RESOURCE LISTS

For those who want a more complete listing of all books, articles, videos, and tapes, there are a number of reference and resource lists available.

Adulthood ADD Lay Bibliography. Compiled by Paul Jaffe. Available from:
ADDendum
5041-A Backlick Rd.
Annandale, VA 22003

Adulthood ADD Professional Bibliography. Compiled by Paul Jaffe. Available from:
ADDendum
5041-A Backlick Rd.
Annandale, VA 22003

Resources for People with Attention Deficit Disorder (ADD) and Related Learning Disabilities (LD). By Marcia L. Connor, Director of Employee Development, Wave Technologies International, Inc.
FAX: 404–947–0303
Voice Mail: 800–994–5767, Ext. 5040
Internet: p00350@psilink.com.

Good resource lists can also be found in both *Driven to Distraction* by Edward M. Hallowell, M.D. and John Ratey, M.D. and *You Mean I'm Not Lazy, Stupid, or Crazy?!* by Kate Kelly and Peggy Ramundo. See "Books" list in this section for bibliographic information on these two books.

Organizations Concerned with Adult ADD

Adult ADD Association

> 1225 E. Sunset Drive, Suite 640
> Bellingham, WA 98226

CH.A.D.D. (Children and Adults with Attention Deficit Disorder)

> 499 NW 70th Avenue
> Plantation, FL 33317
> 305–587–3700

Job Accommodations Network

> A Service of the President's Commission on Employment of People with
>   Disabilities
> 809 Allen Hall
> West Virginia University
> Morgantown, WV 26506-6123
> 1–800–526–4698

The National Attention Deficit Disorder Association (ADDA)

> P.O. Box 972
> Mentor, OH 44063

The National Coaching Network

> P.O. Box 353
> Lafayette Hill, PA 19444
> Phone and Fax: 610–825–4505
> Codirectors: Nancy A. Ratey, Ed.M. and Susan Sussman, M.Ed.
> Send $3.00 for brochure and information.

Newsletters

ADDendum

A quarterly newsletter available by annual subscription by writing to:

ADDendum
c/o Beverly Horn
5041-A Backlick Rd.
Annandale, VA 22003

ADDult News

2620 Ivy Place
Toledo, OH 43613

Attention!

The main CH.A.D.D. publication. It covers child, adolescent, and adult ADD and issues and is available by joining CH.A.D.D. For more information about this publication write to:

CH.A.D.D.
499 NW 70th Avenue
Plantation, FL 33317

Challenge

P.O. Box 488
West Newbury, MA 01985

Coaching Matters

A quarterly educational newsletter about ADD coaching. For subscription information write to:

The National Coaching Network
P.O. Box 353
Lafayette Hill, PA 19444

ON-LINE SERVICES

For an extensive listing of on-line ADD services, the reader should refer to *Resources for People with ADD and LD,* by Marcia L. Connor, listed in "Adult ADD Resource Lists" in this section.

America On-line: There is an adult ADD support room where adults with ADD share support and information. For more information, send E-mail to: ERICNJB@AOL.COM.

CompuServe: Look up GO ADD. For more information, send mail to: 70006.101@compuserve.com.

Listservs: Includes numerous Internet discussion lists on various topics pertaining to ADD.

Prodigy: Adult ADD support groups are listed under: Support Groups Medical.

TAPES AND VIDEOS

Many adults with ADD may prefer to use tapes or videos instead of books. Tapes have been made of many adult ADD lectures that have been presented both at the national CH.A.D.D. conference and Adult ADD conferences.

Adult ADD Conference (Ann Arbor, 1993 and 1994) tapes may be ordered through:

Take Two Recording and Duplicating Services
1155 Rosewood, Suite A
Ann Arbor, MI 41804

Tapes from the National CH.A.D.D. Convention (New York City, 1994 and Washington, D.C., 1995) may be ordered through:

Cassette Associates
3927 Old Lee Highway
Fairfax, VA 22050
800–545–5583

Tapes from the ADDA Adult ADD Conference (Merrillville, IN, 1995) can be ordered from:

Repeat Performance
2911 Crabapple Lane
Hobart, IN 46342

Several videos on adult ADD have been produced by several people, including Arthur Robbins, Ph.D., and Russell Barkley, Ph.D. Information about ordering copies of these videos can be obtained through the ADD Warehouse. Call 1–800–233–9273 to request a free catalog.

References

American Psychiatric Association. (1980). *Diagnostic and statistical manual of mental disorders* (3rd ed.). Washington, DC: Author.

American Psychiatric Association. (1987). *Diagnostic and statistical manual of mental disorders* (3rd ed., revised). Washington, DC: Author.

American Psychiatric Association. (1994). *Diagnostic and statistical manual of mental disorders* (4th ed.). Washington, DC: Author.

Comings, D. E. (1990). *Tourette syndrome and human behavior.* Duarte, CA: Hope Press.

Copeland, E. D. *Copeland symptom checklist for adult attention deficit disorders.* Atlanta: Southeastern Psychological Institute.

Gerber, P. J., Ginsberg, R., & Reiff, H. (1992). Identifying alterable patterns in employment success for highly successful adults with learning disabilities. *Journal of Learning Disabilities, 25* (8), 475–487.

Gordon, M. (1986). How is a computerized attention test used in the diagnosis of attention deficit disorder? *Journal of Children in Contemporary Society, 19* (1–2), 53–64.

Grant, D. A., & Berg, E. A. (1984). A behavioral analysis of reinforcement and ease of shifting to new responses in a Weigl-type card sorting problem. *Journal of Experimental Psychology, 38,* 404–411.

Greenberg, L. M., & Crosby, R. D. (1992). *Specificity and sensitivity of the Test of Variables of Attention (T.O.V.A.).* Unpublished manuscript.

Hallowell, E. M., & Ratey, J. J. (1994). *Driven to distraction: Recognizing and coping with attention deficit disorder from childhood through adulthood.* New York: Pantheon Books.

Hathaway, S. R., & McKinley, J. C. (1989). *Minnesota Multiphasic Personality Inventory.* Minneapolis: National Computer Systems.

Hauser, P., Zametkin, A. J., Martinez, P., Vitiello, B., Matochik, J., Mixson, J., & Weintraub, B. (1993). Attention deficit hyperactivity disorder in people with generalized resistance to thyroid hormone. *New England Journal of Medicine, 328,* 997–1001.

Kagan, J. (1966). Reflection-impulsivity: The generality and dynamic of conceptual tempo. *The Journal of Abnormal Psychology, 71,* 17–24.

Kelly, K., & Ramundo, P. (1995). *You mean I'm not lazy, stupid, or crazy?!: A self-help book for adults with attention deficit disorder.* New York: Scribner's.

Levine, M. (1987). *Developmental variation and learning disorders.* Cambridge, MA: Educators Publishing Service.

Lezak, M. D. (1983). *Neuropsychological assessment.* New York: Oxford University Press.

Myers, I. W., & Briggs, K. C. (1976). *The Myers-Briggs type inventory.* Palo Alto, CA: Consulting Psychologist Press.

Nadeau, K. G. (Ed.). (1995). *A comprehensive guide to attention deficit disorder in adults*: *Research, diagnosis, and treatment.* New York: Brunner/Mazel.

Ratey, J. J., Hallowell, E. M., & Miller, A. C. (1995). Relationship dilemmas for adults with ADD: The biology of intimacy. In K. G. Nadeau (Ed.), *A Comprehensive Guide to Attention Deficit Disorder in Adults: Research, Diagnosis, and Treatment* (pp. 218–235). New York: Brunner/Mazel.

Ratey, J. J., Miller, A. C., & Nadeau, K. G. (1995). Special diagnostic and treatment considerations in women with attention deficit disorder. In K. G. Nadeau (Ed.), *A Comprehensive Guide to Attention Deficit Disorder in Adults: Research, Diagnosis, and Treatment* (pp. 260–283). New York: Brunner/Mazel.

Shinka, J. A. *Neurological symptom questionnaire.* Odessa, FL: Psychological Assessment Resources.

Ward, M. F., Wender, P. H., & Reimherr, F. W. (1993). The Wender Utah rating scale: An aid in the retrospective diagnosis of childhood attention deficit hyperactivity disorder. *American Journal of Psychiatry, 150,* 885–890.

Wechsler, D. (1981). *Wechsler adult intelligence scale—revised.* New York: The Psychological Corporation of Harcourt, Brace, Jovanovich.

Wechsler, D. (1987). *Wechsler memory scale—revised.* New York: The Psychological Corporation of Harcourt, Brace, Jovanovich.

Weiss, G., & Hechtman, L. T. (1993). *Hyperactive children grown up* (2nd ed.). New York: Guilford Press.

Weiss, L. (1992). *Attention deficit disorder in adults: Practical help for sufferers and their spouses.* Houston, TX: Taylor.

Woodcock, W., & Johnson, M. B. (1989). *Woodcock-Johnson psychoeducational battery—revised.* Allen, TX: DLM Teaching Resources.

Zametkin, A. J., Nordahl, T. E., Gross, M., King, A. C., Semple, W. E., Rumsey, J., Hamburger, S., & Cohen, R. M. (1990). Cerebral glucose metabolism in adults with hyperactivity of childhood onset. *New England Journal of Medicine, 323,* 1361–1366.

Index